MEETING COMPLEX NEEDS:
THE FUTURE OF SOCIAL CARE

Jennifer Rankin and
Sue Regan

30-32 Southampton Street
London WC2E 7RA
Tel: +44 (0)20 7470 6100
Fax: +44 (0)20 7470 6111
info@ippr.org
www.ippr.org
Registered charity 800065

New Loom House
101 Backchurch Lane
London, E1 1LU
Tel: +44 (0)20 7702 2300
Fax: +44 (0)20 7702 1456
www.turning-point.co.uk
Registered charity 234887

The Institute for Public Policy Research (ippr), established in 1988, is Britain's leading progressive independent think tank. The values that drive our work include delivering social justice, deepening democracy, increasing environmental sustainability and enhancing human rights. Through our well-researched and clearly argued policy analysis, our publications, our media events, our strong networks in government, academia and the corporate and voluntary sector, we play a vital role in maintaining the momentum of progressive thought.

ippr's aim is to bridge political divide between the social-democratic and liberal traditions, the intellectual divide between academia and policy making, and the cultural divide between the policy-making establishment and the citizen. As an independent institute, we have the freedom to determine our research agenda. ippr has charitable status and is funded by a mixture of corporate, charitable, trade union and individual donations.

For further information you can contact ippr's external affairs department, info@ippr.org, see our website www.ippr.org and you can buy our books from Central Books, tel +44 (0)845 458 9910 or through www.centralbooks.com.

Turning Point is the UK's leading social care organisation providing services for people with complex needs across a range of health and disability issues. It is the largest provider of substance misuse treatment services and a major provider of mental health and learning disabilities services. Last year, Turning Point had contact with almost 100,000 people through services in 200 locations across England and Wales. Since our first service was opened in 1964, we have continually developed new expertise and found innovative solutions that turn lives around for individuals and communities.

For further information you can contact Turning Point's communications team: info@turning-point.co.uk or visit our website at www.turning-point.co.uk

Turning Point is a registered charity, no 234887, a registered social landlord and a company limited by guarantee no 793558 (England & Wales).

Production & design by **emphasis-publishing.co.uk**
ISBN 1 86030 240 8
© IPPR 2004

Contents

Acknowledgements

This publication has been a partnership between ippr and Turning Point. In particular, the authors are grateful to Victor Adebowale, Caroline Hawkings, David Hoare, Richard Kramer, Caitlin Milne, Beverley Priest from Turning Point; Laura Edwards, Nick Pearce, Deborah Roche, Helena Scott, Peter Robinson from ippr for their valued input and advice. In addition we would like to thank Liz Kendall who developed the project at ippr, and gave ongoing support after taking up her new position at the Maternity Alliance. We are also grateful to Harry Cronin, at County Durham Darlington Priority Services NHS Trust, who provided extremely valuable feedback on an early draft.

The project would not have been possible without the support of Turning Point service managers. We would especially like to thank John Campbell and David Morrin for facilitating the meetings with service users so effectively. ippr is very grateful to all the service users who gave up their time, and talked so frankly about their experiences with us.

Finally, we are grateful to all those who shared their expertise and knowledge in one-to-one interviews, as well as everyone who participated in ippr's policy seminar in December 2003.

About the authors

Sue Regan was Associate Director and Head of Social Policy at ippr until February 2004. She is now Director of Policy at Shelter. Before ippr, Sue worked in the Department of Social Security and at Gartmore plc, and was a founding Director of Elevations Ltd.

Jennifer Rankin joined ippr's health and social care team as a researcher in September 2003. She is currently working on a project on the future social care workforce.

Foreword

Too many health and social care services fail to recognise the interconnected nature of people's needs. For people with complex needs this results in a significant gap in service provision, something that carries heavy human and financial costs. Whilst this government has made an important commitment to joining up public services, it has not been matched by a systematic approach to improving services for people with complex needs.

In this report, ippr and Turning Point set out a strategy for meeting complex needs. Rooted in the experiences of service users, the report puts forward a vision for health and social care services that are truly responsive to people's needs.

There is no single solution to meeting complex needs. Beyond a general cultural shift towards person-centred care, we need specific solutions to meet complex needs. It's time to move away from a standardised 'off the peg' model of care, towards bespoke social care services, especially for people who live in deprived neighbourhoods.

Meeting complex needs is at the heart of two key government agendas: creating personalised services and combating social exclusion. A new strategy for addressing complex needs offers an opportunity to reach those individuals who are not being engaged by existing services. Yet it is not a minority issue. A commitment to meeting complex needs has the potential to improve health and social care services for all who use them.

Nick Pearce
Director
IPPR

Lord Victor Adebowale
Chief Executive
Turning Point

Executive summary

Too many health and social care services are failing to meet people's complex needs. This report – rooted in research with social care users – asks why so many people are still losing out despite the Government's public service reform and social inclusion agendas. It sets out a strategy for promoting the well-being and inclusion of people with 'complex needs' and ultimately all users of social care services.

Understanding complex needs

'Complex needs' is a framework for understanding multiple interlocking needs that span health and social issues. People with complex needs may have to negotiate a number of different issues in their life, for example learning disability, mental health problems, substance abuse. They may also be living in deprived circumstances and lack access to stable housing or meaningful daily activity. As this framework suggests, there is no generic complex needs case. Each individual with complex needs has a unique interaction between their health and social care needs and requires a personalised response from services.

We do not believe that complex needs should function as another service label to determine eligibility, but rather as an active and useful description to highlight those people who need a more targeted intervention from service providers. People's complex needs can have breadth (range of need) and/or depth (severity of need). It is valuable shorthand to describe multiple interlocking problems where the total represents more than the sum.

The gaps in services

Too often services fail to recognise the inter-connected nature of people's needs, namely that people have physical, social and emotional requirements, and that their individual needs are closely related to factors in the wider community such as poverty and social exclusion. Many services tend to focus on people's problems in isolation from the rest of their life. Rather than experiencing a single targeted intervention to meet their whole needs, they receive multiple interventions that lead them on an unpredictable and repetitive journey around different agencies.

The service gap for complex needs manifests itself in two ways. Firstly, there is a gap in health and social care services, which are not designed to respond to whole needs. Secondly, there is a gap in housing and employment services, which are not always integrated into health and social care networks. In addition, area-based initiatives to target social exclusion are disconnected from general social care policy. Undoubtedly, these gaps for people with complex needs are not universal and some health and social care services are very successful in meeting whole needs. Yet examples of good practice serve to emphasise how far some health and social care services still have to go to respond to whole needs.

The scale and profile of the gap

It is impossible to determine precisely how many people have complex needs in the UK today. This is a consequence firstly of the nature of complex needs: the unique interaction between health and social care needs depends on individual circumstances and the fact that people move across a spectrum of need over time. Secondly, there is inadequate data on the number of people who use more than one strand of health and social care services. However, there is clear evidence to suggest that complex needs is a significant issue that affects hundreds of thousands of people and generates high costs of service failure. We have drawn on a range of statistics to illustrate the prevalence of the component parts of complex needs (mental health, substance misuse, learning disability statistics, etc) and used case studies to indicate the inefficiency of failing to meet whole needs.

Some people are at greater risk of experiencing complex need than others. Age, ethnicity and socio-economic status are all likely to increase the likelihood of having complex needs and of experiencing service failure.

In general, there is a clear need for better information on people who use multiple services. We recommend that government introduces a statutory duty on the NHS and local authorities to establish a tracking system to monitor the number of service interventions that each individual receives. In the long term this should lead to a more precise understanding of complex needs and will help inform more effective commissioning, and ultimately provide an inter-connected response for individuals.

Vision for meeting complex needs

The broad principles that should drive what people can expect from social care services are:

- *Whole Needs:* An approach of understanding 'the whole person' rather than a single problem should become embedded in every stage of service delivery, from assessment and treatment to aftercare;

- *Creative Whole Systems Services:* Rather than relying on average 'off the peg' methods, service providers need to be encouraged to be flexible and creative in their response to people;

- *Single Point of Entry:* Users of all public services should be able to access an entire system of integrated support through a single point of entry;

- *User Empowerment:* Users of social care services need to be recognised as equals and co-producers in their own care. The agenda of user empowerment cannot stop at the care of the most vulnerable.

The Government is moving away from narrow performance indicators towards broader core standards, which are expected to go live in 2006. These new core standards should reflect a commitment to meeting complex needs and should operate consistently across health and social care.

Towards personalised public services

Although the founders of social service envisaged 'a door on which everyone could knock', successive generations of policy makers have struggled to implement integrated, person-centred services. The drive towards personalised services is not a post-1997 phenomenon.

Traditionally, the development of personalised social services has been held back by the formal hierarchical ethos of social care services and low levels of funding in relation to need. In future, government and practitioners need to use the levers of performance indicators and clinical governance to help meet the agenda for personalised services.

Developing mechanisms of voice and choice for people with complex needs (for example, direct payments and independent advocacy) will also help to ensure a person-centred approach is put into practice.

Social exclusion

The concept of complex needs has figured little in the social exclusion agenda. It is has been widely acknowledged that the Government's social exclusion policies have been most successful in helping those on the margins of poverty and exclusion, not in its depths. The next stage for social inclusion policy should be to focus more on meeting the needs of those who are hardest to help. With a focus on housing and employment issues, this report recommends the increased integration of social care into social inclusion policy.

Reforming commissioning

The commissioning process has four elements: assessment, planning, contracting and monitoring. However these functions are rarely fulfilled. In some areas, commissioners have concentrated on purchasing to the detriment of other aspects of their role. Joint commissioning is not as effective as it could be.

The commissioning process needs to be reformed in order to meet complex needs successfully. This entails a clear definition of the commissioner's role as distinctive from the purchasing function. Investment in training for commissioners should help instil a more strategic overview of their role. Crucially, commissioners should carry out a complex needs audit to determine the level of need in their area.

There are several levers that could strengthen joint commissioning. The Government should set a statutory duty on commissioners to integrate their services where possible. Beyond this, commissioners must take action to ensure that commissioning is a more inclusive process. Commissioning should operate on a relational basis, which means involving all stakeholders in the commissioning process from assessment to planning, purchasing and monitoring services. The commissioning board needs to have a genuine commitment to partnership working and collaboration, and the ability to work across different budgets/funding streams.

Diversity in provision

Diversity in provision has been a headline commitment for this Government, but has not been fully achieved in practice. This report explores how to create a level playing field between different providers and sectors to facilitate greater diversity. An immediate obstacle is the lack of information that commissioners hold about what each provider can bring to the table. Commissioners currently have very different attitudes towards the public, voluntary and private sector. From the voluntary sector's perspective, these attitudes are often exacerbated by the lack of financial muscle to negotiate contracts on fair terms. Longer term contracts, the ability to raise funds for capital development and a standard form of contract between the voluntary sector and health and local authorities would all help to create a level playing field. Operating under a strengthened commissioning structure, local commissioners would then assess who provides the appropriate social care mix for their local area.

Structures

Recent years have seen several structural changes in health and social care services including partnership flexibilities, Care Trusts and Children's Trusts. These changes can be placed on a sliding scale from low-level partnership to full-scale integration. Our research revealed that further structural change should not be a priority. The current range of partnership flexibilities and integrated models of working offers an adequate structural framework to meet complex needs. Central priorities need to shift to supporting cultural change that leads to a unified culture of health and social care, and towards developing new models of delivery and new professional roles.

The workforce and effective delivery

A trained and skilled workforce is essential to delivering better social care outcomes. All professionals who interact with people with complex needs should be trained to recognise and relate effectively with people with complex needs. Meeting complex needs also requires a new kind of professional who can help people navigate their way around health, social care, housing and employment services.

A type of 'service navigator' or 'service adviser' could be developed who would have knowledge of all mainstream and specialist services, and who would work with the service user to develop a sustained pathway of care. This role would mean that every individual would have a lead professional to case manage their care, ensuring a coherent package of services to meet individual needs. Among other things, the service navigators would require knowledge of issues such as substance misuse, mental health issues, learning disability, housing, benefits and employment law, as well as an insight into different cultures and the particular problems of people of different ages, offenders and homeless people. They would also have an advocacy remit and help people with complex needs to represent themselves to professionals.

This new professional model should be situated in the wider context of continued cultural change across health and social care. To bring about cultural change, joint training should be extended, with more opportunities for inter-professional training to promote the development of common assessment, treatment and aftercare procedures. Whilst there has been consideration of information sharing procedures for children, this important procedural innovation needs to be applied and extended to adult services.

A new model to meet complex needs: Connected Care Centres

These reforms will strengthen universal services and help to deliver the public service reform agenda, especially developing personalised services. However, these broader changes alone are not enough to support people with complex needs. People with complex needs require a new type of service as well as a new response from existing services. Furthermore there is a strong link between living in a deprived neighbourhood and experiencing complex needs, which is not addressed by existing models of service delivery. As opposed to standardised 'off the peg' services, Connected Care Centres offer people with complex needs a bespoke social care service.

Building on the best attributes of Sure Start Children's Centres, Connected Care Centres would be situated in the most deprived communities and target those who are most vulnerable to experiencing complex needs. This new service model offers a valuable opportunity to close the long-standing gap between the community-based approach and the individualised social care approach. Connected Care Centres embrace the best features of partnership working. The precise model for this 'complex needs service' would be informed by a local needs audit, a feature that should become an integral part of the commissioning process. Although the particular client groups served would vary, the Connected Care Centres would be organised around the common principles of co-location, managed transitions and a single point of entry. Connected Care Centres for people with complex needs sit within the context of mainstream universal services. They would be part of a broader virtual network of care that includes the NHS, local authorities, the police and courts service, housing and employment services. Rather than restrict people, they would facilitate their access to mainstream services.

This new model of delivery enables policy makers to close the gap between social care solutions and social inclusion strategies. Connected Care Centres will have a visible presence in the local community and their staff will be committed to assertive outreach work, in order to target those who are hardest to reach. Furthermore people will be able to refer themselves to the service, rather than being dependent on other service providers to recommend them. The service will be designed and delivered for the local community by the local community.

The need to act

Failure to meet complex needs carries a significant human cost and this alone suggests a new approach to service delivery is needed. Anyone committed to social justice should be concerned when government and society fail the most vulnerable. Our strategy for reform will help extend the public service reform agenda to those who are hardest to reach and deliver social inclusion for those who are hardest to help. Meeting complex needs promises health and social care services that are more effective services as well as more efficient services. Yet, ultimately meeting complex needs is not a minority issue, as it should help transform social care services for everyone.

1. Introduction

The test of a progressive society is the care and support it offers to its most vulnerable members. This report – rooted in research with social care users – asks whether some of the most disadvantaged people in society are still losing out despite the Government's public service reform and social inclusion agendas. We explore whether, and why, this might be the case and set out a strategy for promoting the well-being and inclusion of people with 'complex needs'.

What is social care for?

Social care services make a huge contribution to delivering social justice and promoting equality of opportunity. Yet, the role of social care has long been overlooked by government and unrecognised by the public at large. Whilst a consensus has emerged around the importance of securing the future of the NHS – and improving acute patient outcomes – considerably less attention has been given to social care services. The role of social care in delivering key government agendas, such as tackling social exclusion and reducing child poverty, has often been undervalued (Kendall and Harker 2002).

In part, the low visibility of social care services is a consequence of the fact they have no obvious institutional identity. Spanning local authority social service departments, parts of the NHS, as well as private and voluntary sector agencies, social care services are as diverse as the clients they support. These services include supporting children and families, providing long-term care for the elderly, as well as providing services for people with learning disabilities, mental health problems and substance misuse.

Social care services have long been a poor relation of the NHS, lacking both political prestige and financial resources. Like the NHS however, the network of services has had to respond to continual expansion and rising expectations about what they can achieve. Modern unified social service departments were founded over twenty years after the foundation of the NHS and largely consisted of the branches of services that had been ignored or overlooked in 1948. These services were invested with the purpose of providing social care support for families and communities: the local department would be 'a door on which everyone could knock' (Seebohm 1968). They would provide a safety net for those who otherwise would have no other agency to turn to: in the words of the report, 'it would be the only door and anyone who was turned away would have nowhere to go' (Seebohm 1968).

The architects of social services also aspired to make social care more prestigious and politically important. This ambition was never fully realised and social care services have always occupied a challenging position within the hierarchy of the welfare state. Despite being relatively unimportant and under-resourced in relation to need, they have been charged with delivering social inclusion to some of the most vulnerable people in society. In the last two decades social care services have become increasingly challenging professions to work in, with low levels of remuneration challenging recruitment and retention.

However, in many respects, the outlook for social care services is more hopeful than at any time since the creation of social service departments. The current Government has committed to investment and modernisation of social care: a rhetorical commitment that has been matched by some spending increases to certain parts of social care services. Another encouraging sign for social care services is that the Government has signed up to social care values. A clear commitment to the social perspective, namely, addressing the needs of individuals in the context of their place in wider society, is at the heart of the social exclusion agenda and is evidenced by programmes such as Sure Start and Supporting People. As one commentator has observed it seems that social work perspective has finally arrived, albeit without the social worker (Gilbert 2003).

Complex need and social care

Whilst social care services are clearly playing a vital role in achieving social inclusion for many vulnerable people, there is a concern that some of the most disadvantaged – particularly those with complex needs – are still losing out. People with complex needs have multiple inter-connected needs that span medical and social issues. In partnership with Turning Point, ippr set out to determine how people with complex needs experience health and social care services.

A literature review was undertaken to unravel the concept of complex needs. Through qualitative research with service users, we explored the thesis that there is a gap in service provision for people with complex needs. Participants were in touch with Turning Point, although many of them had been in contact (either currently or in the past) with other agencies from both the statutory and non-statutory sector. A mixture of in-depth interviews and discussion groups were carried out with people with mental health problems, substance misuse problems and learning disabilities. These interviews corresponded with discussions with service managers and a range of other stakeholders.

Service users who participated in the research were aged between sixteen and sixty years, and the focus on this age group is reflected in the overall report. We have not explored the complex needs of older people, although we acknowledge that people's needs may not change significantly at age 60 or 65 (LGA/ADSS 2002). Similarly our report has regional limits: all of the qualitative research and much of the desk research refers to the English experience. Whilst the report offers parallels to the devolved nations, it offers no commentary on issues that may be distinctive to their health and social care services.

Although this report has a particular focus on people with complex needs, instituting these changes throughout all services ought to transform the experience of social care for everyone who uses them. Social care services need to be understood within the framework of 'targeted universalism': universally supported social care services available for all who need them, with intensive levels of support for people who need them most, such as people with complex needs.

This report, and associated research, seeks to answer whether the Government's public service reform and social inclusion strategies are reaching people with complex needs. Part I sets out a framework for understanding complex needs, explores the nature of the gap in service provision and gives an indication of the scale of the problem of unmet need. Part II considers the current policy landscape and underlines that meeting complex needs will contribute to achieving two key government agendas, namely modernising public services and reducing social exclusion. Part III considers the factors within social care services that have inhibited meeting complex needs in the past and details solutions that will enable services to meet those needs in the future. The report concludes with a strategy for reform to achieve this goal.

I: Complex needs

Jane
Jane is 24 and has suffered from bouts of depression since her early teens. She has also self-harmed in the past. She hints at a history of abuse and has spent time in children's home. She also has a drink problem and describes herself as a binge drinker, although she is now getting the problem under control. She has no permanent place to live at the moment and has been living on a friend's floor for the last year. Her relationship with her family has broken down.
Complex = depression, alcohol abuse, housing problem, family breakdown, history of abuse

Helen
Helen is studying for her A-levels; she is withdrawn and suffers from depression. Doctors also suspect that she has Asperger's Syndrome, which is characterised by impairment in social interaction and the development of restricted and repetitive patterns of behaviour, interests and activities.
Complex = depression and potential learning disability

Ian
Ian is homeless and has been using heroin for over six years. Now 27, he is registered as disabled because of his substance abuse problem. He has spent time in prison and received drug intervention treatment but has not kept clean outside. He suffers from depression, which he says is caused in part by his partner leaving him whilst he was in prison, taking their child with him. He lacks the motivation to come off drugs, which he steals to pay for and doesn't know how he'd go about getting a job with a criminal record.
Complex = homeless, substance addiction, criminal activity, depression, homelessness, family breakdown, no job
'I've just got out of prison, I got straight back on the gear again, 'cos my missus, my kids, everything had gone, basically I need help, I need somewhere to live 'cos I'm homeless, I need help with everything at the moment'

Martin
Martin is in his early forties and has a partner and two young children. He is diagnosed as schizophrenic but also has a history of alcohol abuse and, at times, violent behaviour. His partner is also in touch with mental health services and their children have previously been on the 'at risk' register.
Complex = mental health problem, history of substance misuse, family situation

Karen
Karen is in her late 30s and has a learning disability classified as 'severe'. Over the years she has been in touch with a wide range of service providers and has often been labelled as 'challenging' or as having a 'behavioural problem'. She gets frustrated and sometimes aggressive which means that services are sometimes unable to 'deal' with her. She will require some support throughout her life.
Complex = learning disability classified as severe, coupled with 'challenging' behaviour

Sharon
Sharon has schizophrenia and has demonstrated suicidal tendencies in the past. She also has an eating disorder; depression and a rare sleeping disorder. She has a history of abuse as a child. Sharon has a long history of contact with health and social care services.
Complex = long history of multiple mental health problems coupled with a range of health needs

(Edwards 2003)

2. Understanding complex needs

On one level everyone has complex needs. Nobody has just one single
need; everyone needs a secure source of income, a suitable place to live,
meaningful activity and social interaction. Our understanding of
complex needs is that people have multiple inter-connected needs that
span medical and social issues. People with complex needs may have
mental health problems, combined with substance abuse disability,
including a learning disability. At the same time they may be
experiencing social exclusion, such as living in poor housing, with few
opportunities for meaningful activity and leisure.

We have chosen to present complex needs as a framework for
understanding the inter-connected nature of people's needs, rather than
a carefully controlled definition. Above all, as the cited case studies
show (from ippr's qualitative research), there is no typical complex
needs case. Thus the search for a definitive label is neither meaningful
nor useful to professionals, who in the past have discovered that overly
prescriptive definitions can be difficult to apply in practice. This
framework of complex needs also aims to capture the fact that different
people respond in different ways to a similar situation; an issue that is
complex in one person's life, may be managed by somebody else.

The breadth and depth of complex needs

'Complex needs' is a term that practitioners have used loosely in the
past. Sometimes it is employed to describe people with multiple
problems; at other times it is shorthand used to summarise those who
are hardest to help, such as people with challenging behaviour or severe
substance misuse problems. Our discussions with Turning Point's
service managers reveal that there is uncertainty about the term: are
people's needs complex because services are unable to meet them fully
or are services not working effectively because people's needs are
complex?

Our research starts with the user perspective. From this point of view,
'complex needs' is valuable shorthand to describe multiple interlocking
problems, where the total represents more than the sum of the
component parts. The problems experienced by those with complex
needs frequently have both breadth and depth: there is a range of needs

as well as a high level of need. Still, this characterisation needs to be made cautiously: some people fall through the gaps between services precisely because their needs have breadth, but are not recognised as having depth. Each individual component part of the problem may not score very highly on a particular professional register of need. For example, at a young people's substance misuse service, a girl came into contact with services to get help with a drug problem, but also had many other difficult issues in her life: low level substance misuse was combined with self-harm, a recent miscarriage, unemployment, insecure housing and bereavement. However each individual component was not sufficiently serious to merit a response from services (Edwards 2003).

Understanding complex needs is important in several senses. Firstly, it should alert practitioners to the full range of people's needs. Secondly, it should encourage them to explore the breadth and depth of people's need, and the interaction between different needs. Thirdly, it is a linguistic mechanism that highlights a severely excluded group: people who require a more carefully targeted approach from universal services.

Just another label?

Complex needs is presented because it is an active and useful description that should enable policy-makers and practitioners to recognise need. It should not be conceived as the 'latest label' or used to draw an eligibility line between complex needs and 'simple' needs. Rather than the neat binary assumption of simple/complex, it is more helpful to think of a continuum of need that people may move across over time. (Keene 2001). Like other studies, ippr's research drew attention to the fact that people's needs change over time.

> It's important to recognise the different stages of change and progress. You need to know where the client is on the ladder in order to get them towards where you want them to be.
>
> Service manager (Edwards 2003)

Definitions and service labels have often been used to establish strict institutional boundaries within health and social care services. For this reason they can attract controversy. For example, many clinicians have difficulty with diagnoses such as personality disorder. Dual diagnosis is also a diagnostic label that attracts more criticism than favour (Robbins 2000, Peterson 1998). A more detailed examination of dual diagnosis is useful, however, as it reveals the problems of meeting more than one need.

Dual diagnosis

Dual diagnosis is a move within the medical community to understand the special problems posed by co-morbidity. It is nearly always presented as a substance misuse problem co-existing with a serious mental health problem. (Occasionally it is used to describe a mental health problem co-existing with learning disability (Robbins 2000).) Originally imported from the United States, this diagnostic tag is now well recognised. As the Department of Health notes 'substance misuse is usual rather than exceptional amongst people with severe mental health problems and the relationship between the two is complex' (Department of Health 2002a). Dual diagnosis is a phrase that echoes through the demarcation debates between mental health and addiction services. Clinicians have made a strong case for why co-morbidity needs special treatment, beyond standard procedures (Robbins 2000). People diagnosed with dual diagnosis have a poorer prognosis, higher relapse rate and higher level of non-compliance with services (Keene 2001).

The two disorders of substance abuse and mental health show many similarities: extreme behaviour, denial, vulnerability to relapse, an inattention to physical health and a negative impact on the family and carers (Watkins 2001). However, although the symptoms may be the same, the means of understanding them are very different and inhibit an integrated approach. Dual diagnosis is a useful clinical tool for treating co-morbidity, but it is a limited tool in helping to meet people's whole needs. Inbuilt into the diagnosis are two flawed assumptions: firstly, that a client only has medical needs and secondly, that they only have two needs. It does not alert clinicians to the importance of dealing with people's social and emotional needs (Rassool 2002, Boyd 1999). Some practitioners find the concept wholly unhelpful; a qualitative study of some substance misuse workers revealed that many felt that managing mental health issues, including depression, anxiety and other disorders was a near universal issue and not one peculiar to one particular group (Weaver and Ritter 1999). It was also believed that such 'definitions' had the effect of excluding clients from services (Watkins 2001, Weaver and Ritter 1999).

There is uncertainty as to how serious each half of the diagnosis has to be before it constitutes dual diagnosis. Some practitioners have drawn up typologies of complex needs according to which problem came first and how serious the problems are. These typologies try to explain whether substance abuse is always addiction and point to when low level drug abuse becomes problematic and whether common mental health disorders, such as depression or anxiety, count as mental illness in the framework of dual diagnosis. Others believe – because of the inter-relationships between different problems – that this exercise has as much precision as deciding whether the chicken or the egg came first.

The Department of Health guidelines on dual diagnosis provide some resolution of these issues. Acknowledging the complexity of definitions, the guidelines focus on those people with high substance misuse and serious mental health problems. For example, they differentiate between 'an individual with schizophrenia who misuses cannabis on a daily basis to compensate for social isolation' and 'a dependent drinker who experiences increasing anxiety' (Department of Health 2002). However, this framework reinforces the misleading view that complex problems are always deep, rather than wide-ranging. People with complex needs can fall at either end of the spectrum. Thus, although dual diagnosis represented an important change within the medical profession, it is no substitute for a genuine approach to meeting whole needs.

3. The nature of the gap

Within government there is growing recognition of inter-related needs and a clear commitment to tackling discrimination and social exclusion, as well as improving opportunities in education, work and housing, for people in touch with social care services (see for example *Valuing People* (2001), *Modernising Mental Health Services* (1998), and *The National Service Framework for Mental Health* (1998)). A number of reforms are highly relevant to people with complex needs, such as moving to a person-centred planning approach in learning disability, preventing the social exclusion of people with mental health problems and taking a harm reduction approach with substance misuse.

Yet whilst there is recognition of the joined up nature of people's needs, this does not always translate into practical strategies to address those needs. Our and others' research with service users shows that too often services fail to recognise the inter-connected nature of people's needs, namely that people have physical, social, and emotional requirements, and that their individual needs are closely related to factors in the wider community, such as poverty and social exclusion (see Kendall and Harker 2002, Keene 2001, Social Exclusion Unit 2002).

There are many good and excellent services that are leading the way towards a more person-centred, holistic approach for people with some complex needs (examples of good practice are showcased in Chapter 9). However, the incidence of service failure has revealed itself in two key areas. First, there is a gap within health and social services, which are frequently not designed to respond to people's whole needs. Second, there is a gap in housing and employment services, and how these work with social care agencies to support people with complex needs.

The people left behind, who remain removed from society and disengaged from current services, are often those with the most complex or challenging needs. This phenomenon has been described as the 'inverse care law': the more complex a person's needs, the more likely they are to fall between the gaps in the services society provides. It is also worth pointing out that people whose multiple needs are not necessarily severe often lose out; it would seem it is the complexity rather than severity of need that means people get inappropriate services.

Health and social care services

Health and social care services were designed to meet single rather than multiple needs: each individual service branch – whether mental health, substance addiction or learning disability – has grown up with a fixed idea of what constitutes their 'core business'. Thus, there is an inbuilt inflexibility about meeting the full range of people's needs. As a result, people are often not assessed or treated in relation to their whole needs. Different services have very different starting points for treatment, methods of treatment and definitions of success. As a result of these countervailing philosophies, people in touch with mental health services may find that those services are reluctant to explore or offer support with a substance misuse problem (Weaver and Ritter 1999). Likewise they may get in touch with drug and alcohol services, where staff lack the skills in dealing with mental health issues, or refuse to deal with the mental health problem until the individual has successfully overcome their substance addiction (Rassool 2002).

> I went to this place where people go when they have mental health breakdowns, depression and stuff. They have someone to talk to and all that and if you need prescription medication they can do that. I've been there, sat in a room, talked to a doctor and what not and she prescribed Prozac [...] But when it come to the gear and all that, they didn't want to know, they weren't interested. I told them straight, I don't mind telling anyone.
>
> Service user (Edwards 2003)

Many services have a tendency to focus on people's problems in isolation from the rest of their life. Rather than experiencing a single targeted intervention to meet their whole needs, they receive unconnected multiple interventions that lead them on an unpredictable and repetitive journey around different agencies. As ippr's research shows, 'different service providers chip away at different parts of the problem but don't always join up to maximise their impact' (Edwards 2003). Among service users this breeds a sense of frustration that they are not getting the help that they want to achieve their aims, whether that is beating addiction, finding a job or securing a safe place to live (Edwards 2003, Revolving Doors Agency 2003a).

Within health and social care services there is a lack of support about managing day-to-day life, such as paying bills or accessing financial support. Providing support with these non-health issues is viewed as an optional extra, even though these optional extras may be essential to ensuring successful outcomes. Professional training and identity encourage practitioners to concentrate on the core business of mental health or substance addiction. Resource pressures and government targets can contribute to this tendency. It is understandable that service providers want to focus on what they are good at, but this can also mean a lack of creativity as practitioners take refuge in the comfort of routine procedures. For example people with learning disabilities attending a day service may find they receive a standard 'off-the-peg' service where each day follows the same routine and everyone does the same thing (Edwards 2003, Heyman *et al* 2004, Morris 2000). As many providers have discovered themselves, this is not what people want from the service. Similarly, mental health services are dominated by standard medical treatments and there is a reluctance to explore alternative therapies or counselling, which could be more effective with some clients (Edwards 2003, Repper 2001).

The problem not only lies in the type of support, but the speed at which it is offered. In the statutory sector the path to treatment is not always quick enough for some users, particularly in relation to managing substance misuse. Many people with complex needs have a chaotic lifestyle and making the decision to contact services can be a turning point. Failure to get an immediate response can sap motivation and make approaching services even harder in future. This is a particular problem when people seek help for substance misuse problems. The updated drug strategy shows that service users can wait up to three weeks for an appointment, whilst those deemed 'non priority drug users wait up to an average of eight weeks (updated Drug Strategy 2002). Yet, once a service user recognises they need help, anything less than an immediate response can be a setback (Edwards 2003). It is possible to speculate that these 'non priority users' may be people who have breadth of need rather than depth of need. (It is important to recognise that the National Treatment Agency has prioritised reducing waiting times.)

> They put you on this list and you wait on this list to get an injection from some hospital, they analyse your blood, see how

much heroin you're actually using or whatever and the give you a script of Subutex or something else. But it takes too long, you're looking at a minimum of 3 to 4 months just to get your blood sample sorted and then you've got to wait another few months after that before you get a script of medication.

Service user (Edwards 2003)

Delays can also occur where there is uncertainty about where the funding to support an individual comes from and whether they are eligible for it. Care managers have commented that the time it takes to approach the local authority for funding is too long.

If a client presents with alcohol problems wanting to see me I have to ask them if they've seen the Community Drugs Team (CDT) team and where they are from. Only if they've got the money can I take them. The assessments are taking between two and six weeks and then they'd only be able to come back to me if the care manager agrees. By that time there might not be a bed for them.

Service manager (Edwards 2003).

The service gap continues after treatment has been completed. Despite a rhetorical commitment to preventative continuing care, many services often have a short-term focus (Henwood 2001). Frequently, there is a greater commitment to short-term cures or looking after people in crisis, rather than long term crisis prevention and enabling people to live independent lives. Moreover different professionals have conflicting views of what constitutes a successful outcome; restricted definitions of need can lead to only a partially successful outcome (Harker and Kendall 2002, Revolving Doors Agency 2003a). One successful intervention may be doomed to fail if other issues in the client's life are not resolved at the same time.

One case study illustrates how unnecessarily strict definitions of relapse inhibit a real commitment to preventative care: in an interview with ippr, one woman described how she could not access a relapse prevention programme, until she had fully relapsed (Edwards 2003). People overcoming alcohol or drug abuse may require long-term support and aftercare in order to prevent a relapse.

If I'm supporting someone with an alcohol problem and they get their alcohol problem in control for the care review at three months the care manager may well think that their work is done and they can stop funding the person's place. The client has to fight for longer treatment. If they do manage to fight their case and stay in for longer, they may find they get to one year of being sober and they can manage in their own home. They will still need support in their home to prevent a relapse but the care manager again is likely then to think their job is done and funding will be cut off. There will be no funding for support in the community. If they then relapse, accessing any of the support that they got first time round will be twice as hard.

Service manager (Edwards 2003).

As a consequence of these gaps – that can extend from beginning, during and after interventions – both users and carers share low expectations about what the service can achieve for an individual. Users often find services 'unhelpful' and service workers deem some users 'hard to help'. This 'difficulty label' can be damaging for a client's future chance of successful intervention. Some service users who may have received interventions in the past, which have been deemed to fail, can fall down the priority list for future interventions.

So called 'failed' clients get sent to the back of the queue. With addictions it's not like you're fixing a broken leg. Who picks up the chaotic client if they relapse? There's not going to be a quick change with these people.

Service manager (Edwards 2003)

In general, there is a lack of flexibility about dealing with clients where a traditional intervention has failed. As our universal public services are built on standardised procedures, people with complex needs can be difficult to accommodate into existing frameworks (Heyman *et al* 2004, Glasby 2003). This fact is well documented within learning disability services, where people frequently have significant unmet health needs, even though they are at higher risk of co-morbidity of mental and physical health problems.

The White Paper, *Valuing People,* expresses a genuine commitment to enabling people with learning disabilities to access mainstream public services, but these high aspirations underline what a significant amount of change is still required in practice (Department of Health 2001b). Forty percent of adults with learning disabilities have additional psychiatric and behavioural disorders and also have an above average incidence of conditions such as leukaemia, thyroid problems and skin disorder (Lindsey 2002). One diagnosis often obstructs another, meaning that health needs, both mental and physical are overlooked. Access to primary care is poor, as many General Practitioners lack both the time and training to communicate effectively with people with a learning disability (Keene 2001, Morris 1999). Standardised seven minute slots with GPs, combined with a lack of training in communicating with people with learning disabilities, mean that frequently service users experience an unsatisfactory experience and thus are in effect excluded from universal services (Heyman *et al* 2004). People with learning disabilities also report having their aspirations and social needs overlooked.

An additional aspect of service failure is the inability to respond to people's motivation for their own wellbeing. In ippr's qualitative study many people discuss the importance of their own motivation in order to achieve what they need from services. Yet often the service does not meet their own motivations halfway. In one person's view, self motivation is vital 'if you don't want to do it yourself you get stuck in a cycle.' Although when interviewed this young man remained committed to finding a job and putting a prison sentence behind him, he talked of spells of despondency and used low level substances when this occurred. 'When nothing looks like it's going anywhere I end up smoking' (Edwards 2003). Services are not always good at motivating people and many service users find it difficult to visit an agency that is not responding well to them (Revolving Doors Agency 2003a). Frequently, the absence of a holistic approach goes hand in hand with failure to support a client's fragile motivation.

Housing and employment services

This inability to respond to holistic needs is not limited to health and social care services. There is also evidence to suggest that initiatives designed to tackle social exclusion, in addition to mainstream job and housing support, are not fully attuned to people with complex health and social care needs.

There is rarely specialist help for people who may contact health and social care services. In general, there is little account of problems presented by the same people to different agencies (Keene 2001). Individual case studies illustrate the limitations of services that do not respond to a client's whole needs. One service user describes his experience at a benefits office:

> They just give you the money and that's it, you just get an interview, get your doctor's note and that's it. They don't help you. It's a bit impersonal there, they don't want to know too much about you.

At a key transition point in his life, James was let down by services. His mother died a couple of years ago and he was required to move out of the house provided by the council into a smaller property. He didn't feel that there was any one around to help him with the move and he ended up being asked to pay rent on two council properties at the same time. He fell through the net as it wasn't clear who could help him fight his case with the council and also who could help him physically move his stuff into his new property.

Service user (Edwards 2003)

The job centre can also be a source of disappointment to clients. One client with complex needs had ambitions for a career in leisure and sport. Yet he found support from his local job centre was inadequate; from their database he only had access to a limited number of jobs and was given no advice in making other applications or writing a CV (Edwards 2003). The lack of a holistic needs based approach to services for ex-offenders has been highlighted as particularly problematic. On leaving prison, people may find services provision patchy, even though they are at much higher risk than the general population of experiencing mental health problems, unemployment and poor housing (Revolving Doors Agency 2003b, Social Exclusion Unit 2002).

> They don't help you how I feel probation should help you (ie

with jobs). It's just me coming in and telling them what I've been doing since the last time I saw them.

(Edwards 2003)

Housing services can also not be fully equipped to deal with people who have complex health and support needs. Many local managers feel they lack the skills to deal with people with mental health problems, or mental health workers may not inform the housing department about a tenant's mental health problem for fear that they will lose the tenancy. A series of interviews with service managers revealed that many believed there was a gap in housing people with complex support needs, including dual diagnosis (Boyle and Jenkins 2003). People with complex needs may be dropped into unsuitable accommodation. Two examples from ippr's work include a former drug addict housed in the local crack dealer's neighbourhood and an ex-offender with fears of confined spaces housed in a flat that exacerbated his phobia (Edwards 2003).

The Homelessness Act 2002 does, however, require local authorities to consider housing needs along side care and support needs. The Act places a duty on local authorities to carry out a review of homelessness in their area and develop a strategy that addresses the prevention of homelessness as well as identifying the support services needed by homeless people. It is early days in the implementation of the Act, but initial evaluation (Shelter 2004) illustrates that there is still a long way to go before effective strategic and working partnerships linking housing, homelessness and health and social care needs are widespread.

4. The scale and profile of the gap

Although there is a wide array of statistics counting the components of complex needs, there is a significant lack of information on the incidence of combined need. This is the result of a general absence of inter-agency data and the fact that few social service departments keep records of service overlaps (Keene 2001). The 2003 report by the Social Services Inspectorate observed that within 'the majority of councils there was poor management information and inadequate data on prevalence of need' (SSI 2003). Inadequate information is more than a mere methodological challenge for this research; it is both a cause and consequence of the failure to meet complex needs.

Undoubtedly, obtaining better information on complex needs is challenging. The combination of recurring service use, and potential non-compliance raises challenges for managing information (Keene 2001). Yet this practical issue should not be evaded, as without good information, commissioners and providers will not know the extent of complex needs within their area.

Our research brought to light an interesting case study, which highlights the value of counting multiple service use. In an anonymous county, an information management project tracked use of all health and social care services. Over a period of three years, it mapped the service journeys of 800,000 people. The study found that 22 per cent of users used at least two different clusters of services (Keene 2001). (A cluster was defined as different delivery agencies that comprise one branch of social services, such as learning disability cluster or mental health cluster.) The fact that almost a quarter of service users were in touch with more than one branch of health and social care services has clear implications for determining local need and effective commissioning.

We recommend that a statutory duty is put on the NHS and social service departments to collect data on people who use more than one type of health and social care service. At present, the Government has indicated that tracking service use and making better use of information will become a higher priority in future children's services (Department for Education and Skills 2003). This focus needs to be extended on a strategic level to adult services, in order to have a clear picture of the prevalence of service use.

One way round the lack of systematic data is to count the component parts of complex needs. This indicates that the scale of the problem runs into hundreds of thousands of people, rather than tens of thousands (or millions). Interviews with stakeholders in both the statutory and voluntary sectors highlight there may be many more people who are not in contact with services at all, making them particularly hard to reach. It is also argued that government tends to focus on those people it can see, for example those in contact with the criminal justice system.

- 630,000 adults are in contact with specialist mental health services and over 95% of people in touch with services live in the community [National Institute for Mental Health England 2003].

- 210,000 people have severe/profound learning difficulties, including 25,000 children and young people, 120,000 adults of working age and 25,000 older people [Department of Health (2001) Valuing People].

- There are 250,000 class A drug users, who account for 99% of the costs of drug misuse in England & Wales [Updated Drug Strategy 2002].

- *Dual diagnosis:* It is estimated 30% of people with mental health problems also have drug or alcohol problems [Sainsbury Centre for Mental Health 2003].

- One sixth of presentations to Accident and Emergency wards are the result of alcohol problems or addiction [Strategy Unit 2002].

- 72% of male and 70% of female sentenced prisoners suffer from two or more mental health disorders.

- 66% of male sentenced prisoners and 55% of female sentenced prisoners have used drugs in the year before imprisonment.

- 63% of male sentenced prisoners and 39% of female sentenced prisoners have been classed as hazardous drinkers in the year before imprisonment [Social Exclusion Unit (2002) Reducing Reoffending by Ex-Prisoners].

- 60, 800 children are in local authority care in 2003 [Department of Health 2003].

- 43% of 5-17 year olds in local authority care were diagnosed as having a mental disorder [Department of Health 2003].

- 9,535 pupils were permanently excluded from maintained schools in England in 2001-2 [Department for Education and Skills 2003].

- 920,000 children live in families where one or both parents have a problem with alcohol [National Association for Children of Alcoholics 2003].

Some people are at greater risk of experiencing complex needs than others. Age, ethnic background and socio-economic status are factors that increase the likelihood of having complex needs and experiencing service failure. In addition, there is a heightened risk at key transition points in life; such as becoming an adult or a pensioner, leaving prison or the armed services. None of the groups highlighted here cause any surprises. They stand out because services have traditionally been ill-prepared to meet their needs or because they are more likely to experience multiple inter-locking problems.

Children and young people

Protecting children at risk has become a prominent issue in recent policy discussions. The publication of *Every Child Matters* (Department for Education and Skills 2003) marked a fresh commitment to offering young people a joined up response from services. In many respects, this Green Paper showed a strong understanding of the need for an inter-connected response to children's needs.

However, some commentators have judged that the place for teenagers within Children's Trust has not sufficiently developed (Edwards and Hatch 2003). If the vision for children's services is to be realised it is essential to smooth out gaps between different age services. When commenting on their experience, young service users have drawn attention to the lack of help they receive at the point of transition to adult-based services. Reaching the age of 16, 18 or 19 can mean services abruptly switch off, which families have likened to 'disappearing into a void' (Edwards 2003, Morris 1999).

Older people

As with the young, older people can also be vulnerable to abrupt service transitions. Whilst their needs may not necessarily change at age sixty or sixty-five, access to services can diminish. In a survey conducted by Age Concern, over three quarters of GPs confirmed that age-based rationing occurred in the NHS. As the Association of Directors of Social Services (ADSS) has highlighted, there is a tendency among the rest of society and younger people to think of 'the elderly as a separate group – just because we are older doesn't mean our needs fundamentally change' (ADSS 2002).

Women

Women also have a distinctive experience of services. Government guidelines note that women tend to access services later than men, and with a more severe presentation: 'the complexity and severity of need among women with a dual diagnosis requires the development of tailored services that are both attractive to women and relevant to their needs.' (Department of Health 2002a). Women diagnosed with substance misuse and mental health problems are also more likely than men to have experienced sexual and emotional abuse. Yet fear of losing their children may deter them from approaching services (Watkins 2001). Recently, there has been a new awareness of the impact of gender differences on health outcomes. Extending gender analysis to social care would be a useful area for further research.

Black minority ethnic communities

It is now well known that some minority ethnic service users have had negative experience of mainstream health and social care services (Department of Health 1998a). In particular, mental health services often fail to meet the needs of Afro-Caribbean males (Sainsbury Centre for Mental Health 2002, Greatley and Ford 2002). Afro-Caribbean men are more likely to experience a restrictive care regime, such as compulsory admission under statutory compulsion, and also more likely to have police involvement in their care. In assessment, they have a higher chance of a diagnosis of schizophrenia and a lower chance of being diagnosed with depression. In treatment they are more likely to be prescribed psychotropic medicine and less likely to receive alternative therapies treatments. Carers have felt ignored and interviews with mental health staff have also shown that some are uncertain about engaging with ethnic minority patients. A Sainsbury Centre survey drew the conclusion that many black service users had a traumatic experience in acute care settings and that interactions were frequently confrontational (Sainsbury Centre for Mental Health, 2002). In early 2004 the treatment of black patients in the NHS mental health services came to the foreground, when an inquiry into the death of a black patient in psychiatric care concluded there was institutional racism in the NHS. This specific finding was not supported by the Government (*The Guardian* 12.02.2004).

Across the public services, there are ongoing efforts to combat in-built service discriminations. Yet much remains to be done to ensure that this becomes an area where service providers deliver equality rather than simply discuss it. There is a danger that commitment to equality of outcome becomes axiomatic rather than bringing effective change.

Homeless people

People who are homeless or in vulnerable accommodation also have a higher than average risk of complex needs. The chaotic, rootless nature of life on the street or the insecurity of living in temporary accommodation means it is easier to fall through existing services or to lose contact with services altogether.

It is difficult for homeless people to link up with mainstream statutory care systems, especially if they have a substance misuse problem (Homeless Link 2003b). One study indicated that homeless people with mental illness and substance dependency are five times as likely to lose contact with caring agencies as those who were not similarly dependent (Keene 2001).

Ex-offenders

As numerous studies have shown offenders have a significantly higher possibility of experiencing mental health problems, substance misuse and social exclusion. Prisoners and ex-offenders face a high probability of moving through a revolving door from prison to release and back again. One London-based voluntary organisation found that 60 percent of offenders who came into contact with them, experienced a decline in housing quality three months prior to offending (Revolving Doors Agency 2003b). Problems are particularly acute for people on remand, a status which means are unable to access some drug treatment services. Short-stay prisoners who complete the majority of their time on remand find services on release even less integrated. The majority of remanded young men are held in custody for a relatively short period and little is done to address their needs in prison or to help them mend their disrupted lives on release (Howard League for Penal Reform 2003).

Pathways through care

Our research with service users highlighted the complicated and disrupted pathways through care that people with complex needs often experience. After a number of disconnected interventions, individuals are often no better off than when they first approached a service or authority for help.

People with complex needs are often the easiest people to ignore. Frequently they are the least willing and least able to articulate their needs. Service users who do manage to access services speak of the necessity of persistence in order to access the help they need; people speak of battling against services (Edwards 2003).

Overcoming the range of barriers to meeting complex needs must build from a vision of what should be expected from social care services for people with complex needs, and be seen in the context of the current policy landscape to reform public services and tackle social exclusion.

II: The policy landscape

5. Vision and guiding principles

A vision for people with complex needs

Based on the experiences of users, we highlight the essential attributes of good service delivery. This provides the starting point for what people with complex needs should expect from health and social care services.

- *Whole needs:* Services need to recognise the range of people's needs, namely that people have physical, social and emotional needs. Understanding 'the whole person' rather than the single problem is an approach that needs to become embedded in every stage of service delivery from assessment, treatment to aftercare. People should have a joined-up assessment of their whole needs, which should be followed by a holistic targeted intervention. This response ought to combine appropriate care with practical support in everyday life, such as help with benefits, jobs and housing. Finally support must be sustained after the health or care intervention is complete; services need to take a long-term follow up strategy, with a real commitment to continuing care and support.

- *Single point of entry across health and social care services:* Users should be able to access an entire network of integrated support through one single point of entry. Within government there is growing recognition that people are being passed 'from pillar to post' within the public sector (Department of Health 1998b). However, there still needs to be a more explicit commitment to a single point of access.

- *Creative whole systems services:* Rather than relying on average 'off-the-peg' methods, service providers need to be encouraged to be both flexible and creative in their response to people. The commitment to evidence-based practice needs to be balanced with a flexibility to work with individuals. This means they will need more than one option and a willingness to take risks, with new or unconventional approaches.

- *User empowerment:* The agenda of user empowerment cannot

stop at the care of the most vulnerable. Whilst there is considerable attention given to notions of partnerships between health and social care agencies, the concept of a partnership between service and user is less widely recognised. Yet, in order for care to be truly effective, users of social care services needs to be recognised as co-producers of their own care (Kendall and Lissauer 2001). In practice this means that services need to break down professional boundaries to enable people to manage their own care. In order to reach those who do not normally come into contact with services, providers will have to make use of effective outreach models. The second aspect of user empowerment is involvement within the organisational life of the service; this means active participation on commissioning boards and in the delivery of services.

This vision must be underpinned by some guiding principles: a commitment to targeted universal services, decentralisation, local autonomy and diversity of provision.

Targeted universalism

'Social Services are for all of us.' With this opening statement in *Modernising Social Services*, the Government made a vital commitment to universal social services. At some point in their life everyone may need to call on social service departments. It is clear that social care plays a vital role: in local authorities alone, up to 1.5 million people are in touch with services at any one time (Department of Health 1998a). Yet although social care services need to be readily available to everyone, some people will have a more sustained need for care and support. Social care services are universalist rather than universal; social care services are not universally experienced, neither are other major public services such as health or education (Timmins 2001). People with complex needs require a more focused and intensive support from universal health and social care services. Similarly, the reform of children's services set out in *Every Child Matters* operates within this framework; Children's Trusts will offer a high quality universal service for all children, with specially targeted interventions to those most at risk (Department for Education and Skills 2003).

Decentralised locally-based services

However, universalism should not mean universally alike services. The current trend in health services is towards greater decentralisation, with Primary Care Trusts now controlling up to three quarters of budgets and foundation trusts scheduled for April 2004. Foundation trusts are the most prominent commitment to decentralisation in health and social care. Some have expressed concern that decentralisation is not compatible with equity and may be at odds with complex needs. However this danger can be mitigated by clear standards set at the centre. The 'new localist' model describes an approach where central government sets targets about outcomes (national standards and service values) rather than the means of achieving those outcomes (structures and plans) (Corry and Stoker 2002). Ultimately, there is no single delivery model for organising high quality health and social care services, but there are many ways to achieve optimal care outcomes.

Diversity of provision

Local and regional flexibility has been paralleled by increasing diversity of provision. Recent decades have seen the development of a mixed economy of social care as voluntary and private sector providers have played a more prominent role in the market. This report looks at the sectors that are probably most relevant to complex needs, namely statutory and voluntary. It argues that neither sector has the monopoly on effective outcomes or, indeed, service failure.

The voluntary sector has come a long way from its designated role as junior partner in social care services. In Seebohm's words, the voluntary sector will be guided by the social service departments: 'they [statutory services] will be able to tell them where the need lies' (Policy Studies Institute 1989). Voluntary sector providers have argued they have shown the statutory sector where need lies, and that they have greater scope to be more entrepreneurial and flexible than the statutory sector, in identifying need and being able to respond to that need appropriately (Bubb 2003). Frontline voluntary sector workers highlight their own strength as being part of their communities, living in the community as well working in it (Edwards 2003). The voluntary sector has also been judged to have a comparative advantage in meeting the social and personal needs of vulnerable people that are not met by state providers (Billis and Glennerster 1998).

An enhanced role for the voluntary sector in delivering public services has been the topic of much debate in recent years, following the Government's cross-cutting review of the voluntary sector. Our research did not attempt a comparative analysis of the merits of different sectors. Instead, our approach has been governed by a belief that a mixed economy – with different providers operating on a level playing field – should enable commissioners to select services to match local needs. This is explored in more depth in Chapter 8.

6. Personalisation of public services

The Government has given a broad commitment to creating more personalised services and extending user choice, moving beyond a 'one size fits all' approach which can fail to respond to the diversity of individuals' needs and aspirations. For example, *Modernising Social Services* outlines a vision for convenient and timely services that can respond rapidly to emergencies and provide high quality services for everyone (Department of Health 1998a). However, the drive towards individualised services is not a post-1997 phenomenon. Personalised services have been a long unrealised aspiration of public service reform.

Past social services have attempted to grapple with the interdependent nature of people's social care needs, but embedding this vision in everyday practice has consistently eluded them. This failure is the result of distortions at every stage of the policy process; these distortions can occur from policy to commissioning; from commissioning to purchasing; and from purchasing to service delivery. Translating policy into practice is akin to a game of chinese whispers where something is lost at every stage. Part III of this report will outline ways to iron out the distortions at every level.

The 'hidden history' of complex needs

Social service departments were founded with an explicit mission to co-ordinate complex problems and it was envisaged that they would meet the complexity of individual need through joint working: 'because problems are complicated and inter-dependent, co-ordination in the work of social services of all kinds is crucial' (Seebohm 1968). The report heralded 'a more comprehensive approach to the problems of individuals, families and communities [that] should be more effective in detecting need and encouraging people to seek help'. In the creation of social service departments, the 1968 report promised holistic social services that tackled the complex nature of social distress: 'since social need is complex it can rarely be divided so that each part is satisfactorily dealt with a by a separate service'. Although the report was concerned chiefly with the very old and the very young it was at pains to ensure that all individuals would have a service that would be receptive to their needs. Yet in the long run, the ideals of the report were not entirely matched by the practice of the profession.

Complex needs have a 'hidden history': the striking fact is not that social services have ignored that 'problems are complicated and interdependent', but that this credo is accepted and understood, but has never become truly embedded in services. By this, it is not intended that Seebohm's understanding of the complexity of individual need is coterminous with our contemporary understanding of the multiple problems of drug addiction, mental health problems and social exclusion. Yet there have been several key legislative moments that promised more personalised services than were subsequently delivered. For example, the NHS and Community Care Act 1990 aspired to put a needs-led assessment at the heart of health and social care services, and emphasised the importance of multi-agency working. However, there were difficulties putting a needs-led assessment into practice, in part a consequence of needs restricted by eligibility criteria (Parry Jones 2001). Likewise, the Care Programme Approach (CPA) provides another example of the distortions that emerge between policy and practice. Introduced in 1991 for people with mental health problems, it aimed to make a systematic assessment of the health and social care needs of the user, supported by a regular review process and a nominated key worker. However it has been criticised for an insufficient user focus and in practice became a mechanism for review rather than a framework for understanding holistic needs. It was further revised in 1999, when standard and enhanced CPA standards were devised to classify people according to the severity of their problems. Yet as the 2003 Commission for Health Improvement report revealed, the Care Programme Approach is still failing to realise its aims: large numbers of users are not being placed on the CPA and are allocated neither a care plan nor a co-ordinator (CHI 2003).

A historical perspective provides an opportunity to understand the barriers to inclusive social services. Part of the problem stems from the fact that public services lack this sense of history, a consequence of reform being invariably driven by short-term pressures and the need to show results across the lifetime of one parliament. Commentators believe this leads to a tendency to oscillate between two opposing policy positions without sustained commitment. For example, a decade ago joint planning was seriously discredited in the eyes of Labour opposition, but has now come back into vogue (Peck and Glasby 2003). In part, ambitions have been frustrated by the public service ethos and unreformed working practices.

Traditional public service ethos

'Be patient, join the queue, wait your turn, be grateful it's free'. As John McTernan has observed, this ethos, which once characterised the welfare state, is now no longer accepted (McTernan 2002). The traditional ethos of the welfare state inhibited the development of individualised services: public sector practice was legalistic, formal, and empowered the expert over the user. Statutory services were characterised by an adversarial culture where the medical expert 'knows best'. Despite the emergence of the concept of the expert patient, many consultants remain reluctant to involve their patients as equal partners and lack the flexibility to work with their client's point of view, therefore inhibiting the development of a more preventative focus and individual self-management of their own care (Watkins 2001). Failure to work with the client often means that they regard professional interventions as unhelpful and inappropriate (Keene 2001). Interviews with service managers underline the difficulties of overcoming traditional views of vulnerable clients.

> The White Paper – the *Valuing People* paper is actually the first document for thirty years that actually is trying to push services forward and provide any legislation for people with learning disabilities. If you haven't got the legislation behind you, I think the value of people with learning disabilities has never been very high, you know as far funding is concerned, local authority provision, they've always been the bottom of the pile.

> In terms of mental health...you trace it back and how did we get here and you end up in the Victorians. It's all back to the work houses, that's the way people think, it's been set up and it's never really changed effectively (Edwards 2003).

The fact that social care services are not consumed consistently by all individuals, nor across a lifetime, mean that people do not have a reservoir of experience and knowledge to draw upon when they come into contact with services. People turn to social care services when they have reached vulnerable points in their life and as result are not in the position to negotiate the best service for them (Hudson 2000). In addition, despite efforts to move towards a more needs-based approach, there remains no clear criteria for assessing unmet need and a tendency to fit needs according to service eligibility criteria rather than individual totality of need (Parry Jones 2001, Morris 1999). Social care services planned around eligibility, rather than need, can result in a limited response to whole problems (Morris 1999).

Resources

Of course, past failure to meet complex needs was not just a consequence of the public service ethos. Failure to translate policy into practice was partly a result of the significant underfunding of social services in relation to need. Dubbed the 'Cinderella services', social care services had to limit their ambitions to match their funding. Significant underfunding contributed to recruitment and retention problems and encouraged the development of a limited core service. Resource limits have inhibited the development of a truly needs-based service (Parry Jones 2001.) This report recognises the problems posed by long-term under investment, but it is beyond the scope of our enquiry to make a systematic evaluation of the current funding situation.

The Government has pledged significant new resources into social care services (Department of Health 1998a, 1998b). However the impact of these funding increases has been contested. One study suggested that less than two percent of the new money designated for mental health services went into new service development, as most of the increases were swallowed up by servicing debt repayments (Sainsbury Centre 2003). Furthermore, these increases are significantly less than the new funding commitment made to the NHS. Social care services still have a long way to go to make up for the low funding base; some have called for a similar level of new investment as the health service experienced one third growth in real terms over the same five year period (Henwood 2001). Interestingly, increased partnership exposes the challenges of the mismatch in spending for health and spending on local authority social care services. Evaluation of Care

Trusts revealed reluctance among NHS staff to lose the new NHS money into the common health and social care pool (Glendinning *et al* 2003). The reconciliation of differential pay levels for health and social care services should also be addressed in the future, if the commitment to a seamless service is genuine.

As the Wanless report noted, 'further sustained investment in social care is vital because of the current difficulties faced by the social care sector' (Wanless 2002). Supporting this view, we believe a well-resourced service underpins effective delivery for people with complex needs. However increased investment is not the whole solution. Further necessary reforms are outlined in Part III.

Towards personalised services

It is helpful to set out what a genuine person-centred approach would look like. ippr's report, *The Future Health Worker,* set out a vision for patient-centred care that can be usefully adapted to person-centred care. (Kendall and Lissauer 2003)

Person-centred care

Safe and effective
Promoting health and wellbeing
Integrated and seamless
Informing and empowering
Timely and convenient

The Government is moving away from narrow performance indicators towards broader core standards, which are expected to go live in 2006. These new core standards should reflect a commitment to meeting complex needs; they need to move beyond measuring what can be easily counted, and incorporate the quality of experience. To some extent this is already happening across services for old people. Systems to explore user and carer experience are to be established in Primary Care Trusts from April 2004 (Department of Health 2001c). However at present, the majority of health performance indicators are overwhelmingly skewed towards acute medicine (Commission for Health Improvement 2003). We recommend that the new core standards are consistent across health and social care.

At the moment there is a glaring inconsistency in the Government's partnership drive and performance indicator regime. Performance indicators continue to operate as if health and social care were discrete; so that partnerships formed under the Health Act 1999 must disaggregate their data sets in order to respond to separate performance regimes (Glendinning 2003). Instead, qualitative performance indicators should reflect the integrated service that is being delivered. This should give greater impetus to a person-centred approach, as without such internal signals to broader values, there is a danger that person-centred care becomes purely rhetorical. Clinical governance can also help to deliver person-centred approach, but within governance systems there needs to be a more definite focus on meeting complex needs. In addition, other agencies beyond the NHS should conform to clinical governance standards. Such a reformed system of performance indicators and shared system of governance standards would help to focus service priorities and avoid the distortion from policy to practice.

Creating personalised services for people with complex needs also demands greater attention to mechanisms for user empowerment, such as user choice and voice. User choice can be a problematic concept for people with complex needs; it doesn't correspond easily to the compliance elements of social care (Perkins and Repper 1998). Choice within mental health can enable people to access alternative types of treatment, whilst people with a disability have had the option to shape their own service delivery according to their own needs, through the mechanism of direct payments. Direct payments have been shown to provide people with more flexible help, better continuity of care and enhanced quality of life when compared to conventional services (Glendinning et al 2000). However the take-up of direct payments has been very low and has not touched the people who are harder to reach with services, or those who may be subject to compliance or control mechanisms, such as people with mental health problems.

Promoting service user voice can also be problematic. ippr's research with service users found that the role of independent advocacy could be important in providing emotional support and helping people navigate their way through services. Advocacy is a way of ensuring that people who have difficulty making decisions or expressing a preference can participate in decision-making. Supporting the development of independent advocacy services would be one way to strengthen the voices of people with complex needs. The existence of 'a user's champion' should also help users access mainstream services and to be more demanding of them. It would also mitigate against professionals making judgements about people who don't communicate in conventional ways. Although not a substitute for independent advocates, professionals also need to take on more of an advocacy role. People praised services where they found the worker engaged on an equal level. Discussing one provider, one service user commented: 'this isn't so clinical, this is people I can relate to, who I can sit with and talk to you' (Edwards 2003). The skill of getting on the user's side also needs to be developed in professional training (see Chapter 10).

7. Social exclusion

The Government's overall strategy to target social exclusion is necessarily multi-faceted. This project did not have the scope to undertaken a comprehensive evaluation of the many different social exclusion policies that exist, nor assess how they are faring for people with complex needs. Nevertheless, the research provides an important opportunity to offer a broad overview of social inclusion agenda, and through the lens of housing and employment policy, we offer some insights into the success of social inclusion policy in helping people with complex needs.

The concept of complex needs figures little in debates about tackling social exclusion. It has been widely acknowledged that policies to date have been most successful at helping those on the margins of poverty and exclusion, not in its depths (Piachaud and Sutherland 2002). Furthermore, there is evidence to suggest that a neighbourhood-based approach to tackling social exclusion is frequently disconnected from national initiatives that target clearly defined client groups, irrespective of where they live (McGregor *et al* 2003). Regeneration activities have traditionally focused on the built environment rather than the individuals who live in it. Whilst this has shifted in recent years, the role of social services has remained peripheral. Conversely, it is arguable that social workers have focused too closely on individuals rather than their environments. Integration of regeneration and renewal programmes with social care has remained patchy, even in recent years.

A plethora of initiatives, with separate funding streams and distinctive professional approaches has hindered a truly integrated approach to reducing social exclusion. Complaining of 'initiatitis', some local managers have suggested that the number of local initiatives frustrates more effective partnership working, in making greater demands on staff time and competition for funding and clients. In some areas, the relationship between person-centred and area-based initiatives are not strong, and there is neither time nor knowledge to make the connections (McGregor *et al* 2003 Jordan and Jordan 2001). Part III will outline a new kind of service that bridges the gap between person-centred and area-centred approach.

A key strand of the Government's social exclusion strategy has also been to tackle disadvantage in children and young people and thereby prevent disadvantage in the long term. A social care approach has been central to this drive, illustrated in initiatives such as Sure Start, Connexions and the Children's Fund. The focus of our research is adults with complex needs but there is much that is relevant to our debate. For example, Sure Start provides a framework for a wide range of services that are flexible, community based and centred on the needs of children and parents (Harker 2003). These initiatives have not yet been evaluated fully but it is clear that they are endeavouring to achieve a much more joined up response to reflect people's holistic needs.

Employment policy

Employment has been advocated as the main route out of poverty and social exclusion. To date, the employment strategy has helped people get into work who were closest to the labour market and certain weaknesses remain (Harker 2003). Recent work by Save the Children (2003) on severe and persistent poverty and social exclusion illustrates that the Government's strategy is not working well for people who frequently move between work and inactivity. They suggest different policy measures may be required to help children out of severe poverty such as better protection during transitions between work and benefit and at other times of change. This analysis is relevant to adults with complex needs (many of whom are parents) who often have chaotic lives moving in and out of temporary work.

People with complex needs are more disadvantaged in entering and maintaining employment. Frequently, people with complex needs want to work, but struggle to overcome barriers to employment, including prejudice and stigma. People with mental health problems may find the application and interview process overwhelming and also worry about the stigma attached to mental health (St Mungos 2003). It has also been plausibly speculated that badly paid employment may even add to people's feelings of insecurity (Dean 2002).

There is a serious mismatch between opportunities and willingness to work for people with a (physical and/or mental health) disability. Previous ippr research revealed the very complex relationship between impairment, poverty, poor qualifications and worklessness, which translate into barriers to work for people with disabilities (Stanley and Regan 2003). The benefit system also cements barriers to work. People with complex needs may require a longer transition period from benefits to work, and face particular risks of losing income between signing off benefits and getting their first pay cheque.

Many organisations and researchers (for example, Save the Children 2003) have highlighted the limitations of a work orientated approach to tackling social exclusion for people with complex needs. The benefits of work were modest and even 'simplistic targets are at odds with the need to incorporate lengthy therapeutic intervention for problem drug users.' (Dean 2002). Indeed, the dominance of an employment focus to tackling social exclusion has meant less attention has been paid to those for whom work is not the best or appropriate option at the current time. Encouragingly, the Social Exclusion Unit's (SEU) mental health study recognises that 'different solutions are needed for different personal circumstances – for example work will be appropriate for many but not for all' (SEU 2003). ippr's *The Missing Million* report (2003) also stressed the need to consider 'work' as taking many forms, from unpaid domestic work and caring duties to voluntary work to full-time or part-time paid meaningful employment. What really matters is some form of activity; we know the importance of something to do and someone to do it with (Stanley and Regan 2003).

Housing policy

Decent, stable housing is the bedrock of a normal, healthy life and central to social inclusion. Looking back on the configuration of social services twenty years after the publication of his report, Seebohm felt that housing had not been given the priority it deserved. Housing remained poor despite the report's view that it should become the foundation of effective social services (Policy Studies Institute 1989). It would seem that policy makers have under-estimated the need for stable housing. Moreover, it is also now widely acknowledged that housing policy and housing allocation decisions, has led to poor and vulnerable people being concentrated in certain areas. A priority for housing and social policy is now to create more balanced and mixed communities in new and existing developments. In the long run, this will also help take the pressure off public services, including social care services, in certain areas where currently vulnerable people tend to be overly concentrated.

The Homelessness Act 2002 requires local authorities to consider housing needs alongside care and support needs. The Act places a duty on local authorities to carry out a review of homelessness in their area and develop a strategy that addresses the prevention of homelessness as well as identifying the support services needed by homeless people. Extensions to the priority need categories (which guides how and for whom local authorities provide housing) also have implications for people with complex needs. The priority need categories now include a wider range of people who become homeless including 16 and 17 year olds and young care leavers. There is also an extension to people who are vulnerable because of a range of factors including as a result of spending time in the armed forces or prison, or as a result of fleeing violence. These latter categories are not automatically given priority status, but are assessed on a case-by-case basis. The best local housing and homelessness strategies aim to ensure the provision of housing related support services to enable people in all these groups to resettle and prevent recurring homelessness. However, the quality of local housing strategies can be patchy.

The Government programme, 'Supporting People' is an interesting development in the context of complex needs. It provides both a funding mechanism and the opportunity for joint commissioning of services with probation, health and social services authorities. Aiming to support people who fall outside existing client groups, Supporting People combines two funding streams (housing benefit and supported housing management grant) in order to create one integrated care programme. In our research, most of the people interviewed were very positive about the Supporting People initiative, although some put forward the view that communication lines with health services are not what they should be. However, some have questioned whether Supporting People is sufficient: it has been argued that there remains a shortfall in appropriate housing for people with complex needs: 'complexity of need has increased generally, providers of supported housing are reluctant to accept the most complex and difficult clients.'

Supporting People has also been undermined by an inherent tension between its aims of greater flexibility for individual service users and achieving value for money. The Government commissioned an independent review of Supporting People following concerns that the scheme was paying for services that it was never intended to fund. Supporting People was expected to cost £750 million but has already cost £1.8 billion (*The Guardian*, 7 January 2004). The Government has now responded to the review and has made only limited cuts to the Supporting People budget, recognising that significant cuts would destabilise existing services.

Some research also showed that clients were staying in supported housing for longer and finding it difficult to move on (Boyle and Jenkins 2003). Their interviews with key stakeholders underlined these findings: it was felt that housing and care for people with high support needs, especially dual diagnosis, needed to be developed further. Crisis intervention homes were also in short supply (Boyle and Jenkins 2003).

Making social inclusion policy work for complex needs

The evidence available seems to show that the current social exclusion strategy is helping those people who are easiest to reach or closest to the labour market. It is not working well for people with complex needs who are often hard to reach or invisible to services, or for whom work is not the best route into social inclusion.

A number of issues require greater focus if social inclusion policy is to benefit people with complex needs. Paramount is increased integration of social care into the social inclusion agenda. For example, individual care plans should consider housing and employment needs. Our research with social care users also showed that what people often lack is general information and advice about the different areas of their life and well-being. We consider in Part III the role of service 'navigators' that help individuals understand and access the different support, advice and social care and social inclusion services that are available.

III: Overcoming barriers to meeting complex needs

8. Commissioners and providers

Recent decades have seen the transformation of the health and social care market and the emergence of a mixed economy in social care. The Government's avowals to rely on 'what works' underline that the trend towards provider plurality continues. In order to achieve a contestable market, the Government has extended the use of Public Private Partnerships and sought to enhance the role of the voluntary sector. This shift towards welfare plurality has been accompanied by changes in the commissioning process. Legislation of the early 1990s heralded a shift to enabling authorities that commissioned services rather than provided them. As a result, commissioning has become an increasingly complex and specialised operation.

Both diversity in provision and effective commissioning are the foundations for delivering appropriate services for people with complex needs. Yet in practice commissioning is ineffective and diversity in provision has not been achieved. Of particular relevance to people with complex needs is the role of the voluntary sector. There remains uncertainty over the future role of the voluntary sector, particularly regarding its access to stable finance. Despite the emerging status of the voluntary sector at a policy level (evidenced by the voluntary sector compact and FutureBuilders), diversity in provision has not been realised and it is not clear to local authorities when to use the sector. The absence of a level playing field is evident in the lack of a stable source of funding, the absence of standard form of contract with health and local authorities, and 'sudden death' service contracts of between one to three years which inhibit service development and increase bureaucratic costs.

As Part II suggested we do not believe any sector has a monopoly on service success or service failure. Diversity in provision means a level playing field in the commissioning and provision of services but it also requires common standards of excellence and accountability. This chapter discusses the limitations of the commissioning process and outlines how failure to achieve diversity in provision (and a default reliance on the statutory sector) can undermine service delivery for people with complex needs.

The limitations of commissioning

The commissioning process is the baseline for creating effective services. As the Department of Health has noted, effective commissioning is the starting point for improved health outcomes, faster access to services, high quality integrated care, as well as patient and public satisfaction, continuous service improvement and the delivery of national and local targets (Department of Health 2003). It must also be the starting point for understanding the nature of people's needs and determining the quantity and kind of health and social care services required. As shown in the table, there are four spokes in the commissioning cycle.

Needs Assessment – the needs of a population group are assessed.

Planning – services required are planned according to local need and current capacity of providers.

Contracting – services are purchased from the providers.

Monitoring – services are continually assessed on the basis of effectiveness in meeting the needs of the client group and value for money.

Yet all too often the commissioning process is partial and ineffective. Across health and social care community there is a general lack of understanding of these different functions of commissioning. Commissioners lack a clear vision of their role; all too frequently they act as purchasers, or attempt to micro manage providers. In 1968, arguing for social service departments the Seebohm report advocated that: 'research into need should become a permanent feature of the new service' (Seebohm 1968). This unfulfilled recommendation remains timely. Despite being vital aspects of the commissioner's remit, the planning and assessment of need and the monitoring the effectiveness of existing services does not happen consistently (Greig and Poxton 2001). As one former commissioner testifies, many staff in local authorities have little specific training on commissioning (Bamford 2001).

The recent upheavals from Primary Care Groups (PCGs) to Primary Care Trusts (PCTs) have also contributed to the underdevelopment of health service commissioning. There is a lack of imagination about what effective commissioning could achieve and uncertainty about the distinction between providers and commissioners (Sainsbury Centre 2001). Too often commissioners are engaged in purchasing rather than strategic commissioning for need. Commissioners do not spend sufficient time mapping need and communicating with providers about how best to meet that need. A more strategic view of commissioning, as distinct from purchasing, combined with better communications between commissioners and providers would lead to better services for people with complex needs.

Commissioners are also not always prepared to commission for whole needs: for example health commissioners have a tendency to focus on the acute health care sector (CHI 2003). Experts on mental health commissioning also highlight the problems of the primary-secondary care split which means that current commissioning of mental health services is not needs-led or locally based (Light 2003).

Nonetheless, commissioning has not been immune to developments in health and social care towards greater partnership working. The Government has made an explicit commitment to integrated commissioning (Department of Health 1998b). Collaborative commissioning between the NHS and social services has become increasingly common: this is a tool that is particularly effective for low-volume, high-cost services. The Health Act reforms of 1999 provided further opportunities for enhanced partnership through lead commissioning. However, joint commissioning experiences its own unique problems, as a consequence of the distinctiveness of the health and social care traditions. Health commissioning occurs on block contracts, whilst local authority social services are usually commissioned on the basis of spot purchasing (Bamford 2001). Reconciling contrasting funding arrangements can cause problems for providers who are targeting people with complex needs in a flexible way.

> The big problem that we have is that the other day services in the area are block funded so they just get a block of money, whereas we're not. We're 'spot purchase' and people buy sessions here and our sessions are either a morning session or an afternoon session and if we do evening activities then they pay for what ever evening session they pay for. And that actually causes us quite a lot of problems because extra funding has to be found and often there isn't any extra funding.
>
> Service manager (Edwards 2003)

Funding cycles are difficult to align; health is centrally funded, whilst social services are funded through a mixture of local and central government grants, making planning services more complicated. More fundamental problems arise through different professional cultures; healthcare is focused on health outcomes and social care has wider outcomes. Liaison with the voluntary sector is much more significant in social services. These differences can make successful joint commissioning difficult to achieve in practice (Bamford 2001, Henwood 2001). Ineffective commissioning encourages a default reliance upon the statutory sector as well as undermining the commitment to diversity in provision.

The current commissioning process does not support the Government's commitment to diversity in provision. Both the statutory and voluntary sector will need to make changes to ensure a level playing field in the commissioning process, as currently partnerships between the statutory and voluntary sector are not working as effectively as they could be. Despite the fact that many providers and commissioners have a positive impression of the voluntary sector, there are several barriers that block further development of the voluntary sector at every stage of the commissioning cycle.

Voluntary sector providers argue that they are excluded from planning and development of services in the early stages and are looked upon as second order providers by commissioners (Edwards 2003). They are also disadvantaged in the contracting stage. They may lack the high resources to bid for a contract, although statutory sector providers have experienced this as an obstacle to tendering for a service as well. Risks for a small organisation are especially high when there is a lack of clarity on the evidence required to win a contract. Voluntary providers entering into service agreements with local authorities have no standard contract and must dedicate extra time to developing the necessary bureaucratic framework. This is an anomaly given that the voluntary sector compact gave central government and local providers a common legal framework. Finally the sector is restricted to short-term contracts of one to three years which makes it difficult to plan services and adds to the bureaucratic costs. These issues need to be tackled if effective commissioning is to lead to diversity of provision.

Towards effective commissioning

As this chapter has argued, the importance of effective commissioning cannot be under-estimated. Effective commissioning should not become an end in itself, but is the starting point for meeting complex needs. There is a need to develop real criteria for measuring effective service commissioning. Here we outline what an effective commissioning would look like.

● *Clearly defined responsibilities for commissioners*

Everyone involved in planning services need a better understanding of what the commissioner's role is. In the past, commissioners have fallen into the trap of seeing this as purely a purchasing role. Purchasing services is just one element of commissioning. Commissioners need to be aware of the full extent of their role and there should be a stronger distinction made between the overall function of commissioning and the specific task of purchasing, and better communications between commissioners and providers.

● *Commissioners' responsibilities*

Commissioners' responsibilities include: assessing, planning, purchasing, monitoring and predicting future needs. Once the provider has been approved, the commissioner must avoid interference in the day-to-day running of the service, although they can and should highlight its shortcomings and successes. At the moment too few commissioners are aware of the importance of assessing need and monitoring the quality of existing services.

● *Providers' responsibilities*

Providers need to demonstrate how their service fulfils or falls short of the commissioning targets. In order to do this, they must show service quality, responsiveness and reliability. Whether they are voluntary or statutory providers, they also have a duty to engage with the public service reform agenda and government national frameworks.

One clear example of best practice from County Durham and Darlington Priority Services Trust shows what can be achieved when commissioners assess and monitor services in order to plan for future needs. In County Durham, the commissioning board made a systematic evaluation of the quantity and quality of current service provision, identified the frequency of attendance, length of time and level of dependency and then assessed whether existing providers were offering an effective service.

- *Evidence based commissioning and clear commissioning goals*

Commissioners need to know who they are commissioning services for. As the experience of one local authority commissioner demonstrates, effective commissioning only works when commissioners have detailed information about their population group. Although this fact has been known for more than a decade, commissioners do not consistently operate on the basis of good information (Reed 1994). In addition they need to know what kind of service is required. This may require changes in government performance targets to incentivise commissioners to reward providers who meet complex needs. Above all it is vital to have a shared view of what the commissioning process aims to achieve.

Both service providers and users need to be involved in determining commissioning outcomes:

> Talking to staff and service users and commissioners, we came up and realised that people did not necessarily want a five day a week service in place, they wanted different activities and they wanted some form of activities out and about, out in the community, away from the day service.
>
> Service manager (Edwards 2003)

Commissioners need to develop their knowledge of existing providers, as well as of service need. Currently commissioners are not fully aware of their options, as they have limited knowledge of providers. This may exclude some voluntary sector providers and ultimately prohibits the development of the best service.

● *More effective joint working*

In the past ippr has considered how to promote joint commissioning. A previous contribution to the debate suggested that the Government Office for the Regions should be awarded with a pump priming fund to reward joining commissioning by local authorities (ippr 2001). Alternatively, the Government should set a statutory duty on commissioners to integrate service provision to meet complex needs.

Effective commissioning is a cross-boundary process that draws on clinical, social and client expertise. A typical commissioning board would include representatives from the NHS, social services, representatives from the non-statutory sector, housing and employment, users and carers and advocates. The commissioning board needs to have a genuine commitment to partnership working and collaboration. There will be a need for dialogue, avoiding the use of unnecessary jargon.

Both the statutory and voluntary sector need to be treated as equals by commissioners; both should be judged according to the same criteria: assess the service firstly according to its effectiveness for users and secondly, value for money. Both sides will need to take steps to become more effective partners.

Joint funding is a stimulus for a more holistic approach to meeting complex needs. Effective joint working will require clear procedures to rationalise funding streams. The popularity of pooled budgets indicates there is a will to act on this, however providers may need support in working out complex arrangements (Glasby and Peck 2003).

Securing diversity in provision

Beyond commissioning, broader changes are required to secure diversity in provision. The shape of the social care market has serious implications for delivering services for people with complex needs. In Part II we explained why diversity in provision is important, whilst this section turns to how it can be achieved in practice. Throughout this discussion it is important to remember the diversity within each sector.

For example, the voluntary sector is made up a huge range of sizes and types of organisations, and their appropriate role can only be decided locally.

An immediate obstacle is the lack of information that commissioners hold about what each provider can bring to the table. Commissioners currently have very different and contradictory attitudes towards the private, public and voluntary sectors. In relation to the private sector, the outlook is how much we are prepared to pay. In relation to the public sector, the outlook is whether you do it at a cheaper price. In relation to the voluntary sector, the outlook is that this is the price we are prepared to pay – you deliver the service.

The Spending Review of 2002 produced a three year agenda to improve relationships between the government and the voluntary sector: it recommended a more stable funding relationship with less short-term contracts and the involvement of the voluntary sector in the planning and delivery of services. Longer contracts are a simple mechanism to ensure stable funding, but in general, they still do not exist in practice. At the moment, short-term contracts of one to two years inhibit service development as well as access to providing the service in the first place.

The benefits of long contracts would be to recognise that people with depth and/or breadth of needs often have long-term care needs. The high transaction costs of short-term contracts for long-term needs are inefficient. Longer term contracts could lead to better, more thorough commissioning and would encourage PCTs to undertake longer term market analysis. However, too long contracts combined with unsophisticated monitoring processes could lock the market in patterns of provision, and restrict a flexible response to need.

Clearly a balance needs to be struck between stable secure funding and developing a truly contestable market. ippr's Commission on Public Private Partnerships highlighted that a shift needs to be made to service contracts of 1-3 years to 5-8 years (ippr 2001). But this extension would not resolve the sector's inability to access capital.

This has encouraged practitioners in the voluntary sector to look to new forms of accessing capital finance. Inspired by Public Interest Companies, and echoing the principles (and name) of the Private Finance Initiative, the sector has produced the concept of the Voluntary Finance Initiative (VFI). According to its proponents, a VFI would have the potential to increase voluntary sector capacity and reduce delivery costs, without any loss of quality (Peck and Leat 2003). It would have a beneficial impact on the market as whole, leading to increased competition and choice and could reduce pressure on other services. Proponents of the VFI argue that it could have a direct benefit for people with complex needs, by increasing the 'supply of services meeting the long-term care needs of groups with complex needs and in certain politically sensitive and pressing areas such as substance abuse, in which the private sector is relatively weak'. As its advocates acknowledge, VFI does carry potential risks, such as loss of public trust, loss of volunteers and sector distinctiveness.

VFI would allow the voluntary sector to invest in large capital projects for people with depth or breadth of need such as long-term support for people with learning disabilities and challenging behaviour. The sector is not seen as a good risk because of the short-term nature of contracts and the fact that it cannot always receive full cost recovery under existing contracts. Much longer contracts – of 25 years – would significantly increase the ability of voluntary organisations to raise capital in mainstream financial markets for large-scale projects.

The bottom line is that if we are serious about creating a level playing field in the social care market, then ways of enhancing the voluntary sector's capacity to access capital need to be explored.

However, diversity in provision amounts to more than equal access to finance. The advantage of equal access to service provision and capital development will be undermined without fair and consistent procedures to negotiate with local authorities. Many voluntary sector providers, such as Turning Point, believe that a standard form of contract between the voluntary sector and health and local authorities would ensure fair contracts and efficient use of resources for both parties (Turning Point Briefing Paper 2003). Currently, there is considerable variation in contracts between health and local authorities and voluntary service providers.

The problem with non-standard forms of contract means that the contracting process varies substantially from authority to authority and unfair terms are often imposed. The voluntary sector is nominally included in partnerships at a local level. However, any theoretical advantage of being at the decision-making table is undermined by the lack of explicit statement of roles and powers (as not all local authorities have developed a local compact) and a lack of financial muscle by the voluntary sector that would otherwise allow contracts to be negotiated fairly and on equal terms with full cost recovery. Voluntary sector providers believe that the current contractual relationship between local government and the voluntary sector is often characterised by a 'donor and supplicant approach', rather than a relationship based on genuine partnership to deliver better public services.

A standard contract could build on the principles governing the financial relationship between government and the voluntary sector as set out in the Government's original cross-cutting review. It would take account of other precedents that already exist such as the standard contract for Supporting People. It would be important for the voluntary sector to demonstrate that standard form of contracts does not equate to special pleading and that it is about building a level playing field with the public and private sector. Examples should be collated which illustrate how unfair conditions have been imposed in order to articulate the merits of a standard form of contract and the extent to which it will enable future contracts to be negotiated on fair terms. Standard forms of contract also mean that the sector can be scrutinised more closely in terms of price, standards of delivery and quality of outcomes for the user.

The problem with contracting also stems in part from cultural attitudes towards the voluntary sector and the need for better partnership between statutory purchasers and the sector. Cultural changes are more important than further structural changes in the way in which services are commissioned and purchased. However, a standard form of contract is potentially a mechanism to help bring about the cultural change and improved attitudes towards the voluntary sector. It would clear up the anomaly whereby a voluntary organisation has a fixed contract with central government (the voluntary sector compact) but must renegotiate new agreements with local authorities.

If diversity in provision is to be truly achieved, both the statutory and voluntary sector will need to become better partners. ippr's Commission on Public Private Partnerships made several recommendations on how to make the public sector a better partner and how to monitor this. These lessons can also be applied to partnerships between the voluntary and statutory sector. One of the relevant recommendations is to include regular assessment of user satisfaction (ippr 2001). This would be relevant to meeting complex needs but should be complemented with a regular assessment of whether services are meeting holistic needs, and how they target social exclusion.

Implementing these measures has the potential to address the distortions that occur at the commissioning stage. In turn this promises better services for people with complex needs.

9. Structures

In the last decade, health and social care professionals have been buffeted by waves of structural change. These include the abolition of the internal market and GP fund holding, the introduction of partnership flexibilities, the establishment of Primary Care Trusts, and the introduction of Care Trusts. Although these changes have been accompanied by a vision for creating modernised social care, there has been considerably less focus on how to manage change in practice and achieve the cultural changes that are required to deliver more a more positive service experience for users.

In interviews with service providers and other experts, there was more than a little weariness when the issue of structural change was discussed. There was unanimity that 'soft' cultural change issues were more vital than 'hard' structural change. Many expressed the view that the pace of change was unsettling, that it could be disorientating and demotivating for staff, and that new initiatives were rarely given an opportunity to become embedded in services (Gilbert 2003). Other than reforming commissioning structures, few experts believed that further structural change was necessary or desirable. Indeed some thought it would be counter-productive, as it would disrupt the cultural change paramount to improving services. In light of this evidence, this report does not support major structural reform. Nevertheless we have examined the current organisational landscape and assessed how current structures can be developed to meet complex needs.

New partnership flexibilities

The Health Act 1999 was an important step for transition of health and social care services. It brought new freedoms and flexibilities including pooled budgets across health and local authorities, lead commissioning, integrated provision and the possibility of a unified management structure.

Interestingly integrated management has proved less popular than integrated budgets and the most popular flexibility remains that of pooled budgets, either alone or with other flexibilities. In theory, these provisions should serve people with complex needs better as there are greater possibilities to structure services around individual needs. It is not yet clear as to exactly how these provisions will work in the long term. It does seem to have heightened awareness of priorities and increased a willingness to look at new ways of working, such as wider public consultation and new models of joint commissioning (Glendinning *et al* 2003). There remains a danger of a false belief that everything is being provided and a loss of interest from those who hand over power. This could lead to a detachment from other local authority roles (for example housing and planning) especially if the NHS takes the lead (Sainsbury Centre for Mental Health 2000b).

Care Trusts

Care Trusts commission and/or deliver primary and community health and social care services. When announced in the NHS Plan (Department of Health 2000) with minimum detail, the proposed Care Trusts generated concern that the distinctive contribution of social care would be submerged within the NHS.

With only seven Care Trusts in the UK at the time of writing, it remains a limited experiment. The majority of people interviewed as part of the research felt however that the 1999 Health Act flexibilities were sufficient in providing the opportunity for more flexible structures and it was a matter of enacting them well. Significantly, the most effective partnerships already existed prior to the Health Act 1999 or the introduction of Care Trusts. It is striking that six out of the seven Care Trusts were in Health Action Zones and drew on experience of existing multi-agency partnerships (Peck and Glasby 2003). Structures can facilitate partnerships but much more is needed to make them work successfully. The most taxing question is how to create partnerships where none have previously existed.

Children's Trusts

The Government's Green Paper *Every Child Matters* (Derpartment for Education and Skills 2003) sets out their long-term ambition for children's services. Their vision is to integrate key services within a single organisational structure. The Green Paper states that the preferred model for this integration is Children's Trusts and aspires to most areas having these by 2006. The trusts will integrate a wide range of services including children's social services, the local education authority, community and acute health services as well as possible Connexions and Young Offending Teams. Some of the key features of the Children's Trusts will be a single planning and commissioning function supported by pooled budgets and co-located multi-disciplinary teams; an arrangement that will be underpinned by common assessment procedures, protocols for sharing information and joint training.

The Government recognises that it is an ambitious agenda. Some key organisations will remain outside of the trust, such as some health functions and housing departments, and so there will still need to develop close relationships with a network of statutory, private, voluntary and community sector organisations.

From partnership to integration

Partnership has become the new credo of health and social care services. However, it is clear that it manifests itself in a variety of forms. At one end of the scale, there are small-scale local partnerships based around joint commissioning and freedoms and flexibilities. Whilst these remain important, to a certain extent, they have been overtaken by even more ambitious plans for multi-agency integrated working, such as Care Trusts and Children's Trusts.

Clearly, the generic local social services department is undergoing a metamorphosis as the trend to age-related delivery of services undercuts the status quo. In the long-term, the Government has said it wants to integrate key services for children and young people under a Director of Children's Services as part of Children's Trusts (Department for Education and Skills 2003). Some local authorities have already embarked on this 'age-related' approach to the delivery of services; for example Hertfordshire has appointed a head of adult social services and a separate head of children's services. This approach in principle would seem to offer more holistic and joined up approach for individuals, but there are clearly issues when people move through their different life stages. Whilst there is evidence that critical mass can lead to a better service, (Glendinning 2003) the implications of leaving some service elements out in the cold have not been fully explored.

Ultimately, it is important to recognise that there is no such thing as a boundary-less partnership. No partnership can be totally comprehensive. New enhanced partnerships, such as Care Trusts, result in new types of division and pose challenges for the provision of existing services. The concept of the virtual trust has been suggested as one means to overcome persistent boundaries. Some of the Pathfinder Children's Trusts are so called virtual trusts which bring together health and social care agencies, as well as the police, youth offending teams, Connexions and any other agency who deliver for children and young people.

Structural solutions?

It is necessary for governments to overcome the fixation that every problem has a purely structural solution. Structural change runs the risk of becoming a proxy for improved outcomes. It can even hinder cultural change. As one former social worker writes:

> During structural change, people inevitably turn inwards, worry about their own positions, lose contact with some of their networks which bring about positive outcomes for users and carers, and suffer stress and exhaustion. (Gilbert 2003)

Many providers feel that the partnership flexibilities offer sufficient structural flexibility to develop their own services. Therefore, contrary to the Government's agenda which is moving towards greater integration of services, it seems more important to allow recent changes to embed and partnerships the autonomy to develop and flourish. Moreover 'partnership' needs to be understood in its broadest sense, there needs to be an awareness of the value of all kinds of partnership including:

- Partnerships between health and social services, and between these and other welfare agencies,such as housing, employment services, police etc.

- Partnerships between the statutory and voluntary sectors.

10. The workforce and effective delivery

Training and professional knowledge

There has been a concerted effort to pull down the 'Berlin Wall' that divides health and social care. Yet, this wall is more than a structural dividing line. It is underpinned by very different professional cultures, which are shaped by training and supported by everyday practice. Different professionals have different theories, assessment procedures, and reasons for starting help and definitions of success and failure. Although structures cause people with complex needs to slip through the system, arguably it is the different professional cultures that pose greater challenges to meeting complex needs.

The professional oppositions between mental health and substance misuse workers reveal how traditional working practices can undermine meeting complex needs. Different branches of social care professions have very different starting points for treatment. The substance misuse services have developed around the ideals of self-help, individual motivation for change and personal responsibility. By contrast, mental health services traditionally regard their patients as lacking responsibility. Such views have been reinforced by mental health legislation (Mental Health Act 1983) that empowers professionals to detain patients deemed a risk to the public.

Likewise, different professionals hold opposing views on treatment. In one survey, London mental health professionals recorded their ambivalence about their clients' substance abuse problems and 'cure'. They did not belief that the treatment goal of the substance misuse services – abstinence – was likely to help their clients. They were sympathetic to the view that substance abuse was therapy for despair and felt inhibited from stopping this self-medication (Watkins 2001, Weaver and Ritter 1999). There have also been divisive debates between Community Mental Health Teams (CMHT) and Community Drug Action Teams (CDATs) over medical responsibility: sometimes a premature diagnosis of psychiatric disorder resulted from inadequate knowledge of chemical dependency (Rassool 2002). Evidence from America (where integrated substance misuse teams exist) supports this perception of professional antipathy between substance misuse services and mental health. Likewise, challenging behaviour may inhibit entry and successful treatment in substance misuse clinics and this strand of the service is rarely equipped to deal with people with learning disabilities.

Traditionally, these professional antipathies have undermined meeting people's complex needs, and they continue to exert influence on care outcomes. A majority of professionals regarded a single diagnosis as the norm, even if they accept the desirability of a common approach (Keene 2001). Drug alcohol services are often confidential and will not or cannot share information with mental health services. Likewise, they rarely find out about a patient's mental health record. Shared assessment was rare. Productive relationships and close contact were the exception rather than the rule (Weaver and Ritter 1999). From the point of view of a psychiatrist, a successful outcome could mean that the client is capable of moving back home. From the perspective of social care services, the criteria may be to change an individual's life situation: are they in secure housing, do they know how to manage their condition, and how will they be reintegrated into the community (Kendall 2002)? Within these conflicting professional frameworks:

> Individuals who are seen as substance misusers with mental health problems were seen as not wanting help, difficult to treat, unable to participate in counselling or psychotherapy due to the influence of psychoactive substances (Rassool 2002).

The dilemma for professionals is that specialist treatment models can be successful for many patients and there are strong arguments in favour of retaining them. However, such models can potentially distort the treatment of people with complex needs.

Occupational hierarchies and the medical model

Professional barriers have been upheld by the dominance of the medical model, which remains a powerful construct in social care settings. When problems are seen from a purely clinical perspective it may be impossible to respond to complex needs. The medical model remains dominant, despite the development of the social model of disability and understanding of the social causes of mental health problems (the correlation between poor mental health and poverty). Many experts in the voluntary sector believe that medical diagnosis is the start of social exclusion. Simon Foster, head of legal service to MIND, made this point to their inquiry on mental health and social exclusion. 'The fundamental point is that discrimination arises because of the diagnosis, not as a result of the condition itself' (Dunn 2000). Furthermore the medical model upholds other negative aspects of professional culture that can undermine effective outcomes.

> At its extreme the medical model may aggravate, compound or reinforce other attitudes ... social conservatism on issues such as gender, class and race; and deep resistance to change.
> (Salvage 2002)

The medical model is being challenged within health and social care settings, although its influence remains. In new organisations, such as Care Trusts, social care staff have worried that the social care perspective will be lost in a medical environment (Peck *et al* 2001 and ippr interviews). However the existence of combined health and social care partnerships and the increase in inter-disciplinary work and training have the potential to equalise professional hierarchies. A clearer understanding of the purposes of cultural change will enable partnerships to work in practice.

The limitations of the medical model would be mitigated by an increase in the level and scope of inter-professional training. Professionals may also work together more constructively with a shared theoretical framework and cross-disciplinary training (Keene 2001). Training plays a major role in preserving professional cultures. In a survey of psychiatrists in 1999, less than half the respondents had had formal training in substance misuse in the last five years (Rassool 2002). In 2000, the Royal College of Psychiatrists also recommended more training in substance misuse. Some have suggested that all health professionals share a common year of training (Kennedy *et al* quoted in Salvage 2002).

> At the very least all professionals need to be aware of the importance of the plurality of knowledges, and confident

enough of their own contribution and its limitations to allow for adjustment and negotiation (Salvage 2002).

Integrated training is seen as a priority by service managers interviewed as part of ippr's research, in both voluntary and statutory sectors. The shortage of experienced staff was also seen to present barriers to meeting people's needs. In the opinion of one service manager, 'there's a lack of experienced drug workers let alone drug workers who can also deal with mental health issues as well' (Edwards 2003).

All staff who come into contact with people with complex needs should be trained and supported to develop the skills to do their job effectively. They also need to know how their role fits in with that of others and have the skills to work with and draw on the expertise of professionals from other agencies. Training must be provided to support staff in assessing for a range of needs and making appropriate referrals.

Staff need to be skilled in working within multi-disciplinary teams and have the confidence to work across boundaries. They will need to acknowledge the interface between their own activities and those with other organisations and agencies and develop the expertise to make the links between those services already accessed by the individual and other mainstream or specialist services.

In particular, there needs to be a shared level of skills and knowledge across all professions and mainstream agencies that come into contact and work with people with complex needs. A common core of standards and training will promote early recognition of the range of needs across health and social care settings, improve competency in developing inter-professional relationships and help sign-post people to appropriate services. It will also help support the development of integrated services across professional disciplines and promote more flexible career progression across different agencies.

The nature of the common training will depend on the role, level and nature of contact of staff with people who with complex needs. At a minimum, it should provide generic level of training in core knowledge, attitudes and skills in mental health, substance misuse and learning disability. It should equip staff with the knowledge to deal with housing and benefit issues, as well as an understanding of what services exist locally, and how to work with other agencies in order to maximise impact. Some people with depth and/or breath of needs may need extensive and effective support networks across different agencies. Specialist agencies will play a valuable role in linking hard-to-reach groups into mainstream services.

There should be greater priority given to locally based multi-disciplinary training, exchanges of information between specialist and general agencies and the promotion of secondments between staff. This will help to being about close working between different agencies and raise awareness of local issues.

Changing professional cultures

Disillusion with structural change to achieve improved outcomes for users has been supplanted by a new enthusiasm for cultural change. However, experience has shown that cultural change and the development of a 'common culture of health and social care' does not happen spontaneously, but requires a deliberate and focused change in working practices. For example, a study of a Care Trust showed that different staff within the organisation had different understandings of what constituted cultural change. Whilst some believed they were working towards a cohesive culture of health and social care, others had the less visionary aim of gaining a little more understanding between the two professions (Peck 2001). If cultural change is to work in practice there needs to be clear aims of how it is brought about and for what purpose.

The historic inability to deliver personalised services, discussed in Chapter 6, indicates the major challenges posed by bringing about cultural change. Some managers may also hold the assumption that cultural change automatically follows new structures, whilst staff respond to a new initiative or way of working is that 'we do this anyway'. Co-location does not automatically produce new levels of professional understanding and trust. As one in-depth study of the Somerset Care Trust revealed, strong perceptions of inter-professional differences between health and social care staff remained present after one year. Care Trust status brought an overall fall in job satisfaction and a corresponding rise in emotional exhaustion among practitioners (Peck et al 2001). Although it is important to be cautious about drawing firm conclusions from one case study, one important lesson emerges: that it is vital to invest partnerships with clear purpose and have a realistic vision of what it is designed to achieve. This purpose should follow logically from the goals identified by commissioners under a reformed commissioning process.

New professionals

Cultural change is vital to achieve the transformation in meeting complex needs and delivering better services for all users of health and social care. Yet cultural change alone is not sufficient to meet complex needs. A specific focus on new ways of working to meet complex needs is required. The first element is a new role for professionals, which would support people with complex needs to navigate their way through services. This recommendation is reinforced by the findings of several academic studies: one study recommended the development of 'a new type of professional who specialises in complex needs clients' (Keene 2001). Another author advocates a new role for nurses in meeting the needs of patients with dual diagnosis (Rassool 2002).

A type of 'service navigator' or 'service adviser' could be developed who would have knowledge of all mainstream and specialist services, and who would work with the service user to develop a sustained pathway of care. This role would mean that every individual had a lead professional who would case manage their care, ensuring a coherent package of services to meet individual needs. Among other things, they would require knowledge of presenting issues such as substance misuse, mental health issues, learning disability, housing, benefits and employment law, as well as an insight into different cultures and the particular problems of people of different ages, offenders and homeless people.

They would also have an advocacy remit and help people with complex needs to represent themselves to professionals. Some examples from ippr's research include mental health workers who accompanied a patient to a psychiatrist to help them articulate their needs and avoid misunderstanding, or supporting people to access social housing (Edwards 2003). Above all, they would be solution focused by finding out the right form of intervention and support for the individual and co-ordinating the delivery of services.

The navigational worker should not be based in the NHS or social services departments but someone who can work across health or social care services: the voluntary sector can play more of a critical brokering role than a person in the health or local authority. Whilst this new type of professional could fill an important role, it will not bring about the transformation that is needed. As discussed earlier, we should be increasing the skills of the whole workforce.

With overlapping roles in community settings already, one study recommends that nurses may be well placed – given training – to take on new kinds of whole needs roles (Rassool 2002). However, other social care professionals would also be well situated to fulfil this role. This complex needs professional would be drawn from a range of health and social care and educational backgrounds and could be based in the community or supporting other professionals in a range of settings, such as hospitals' Accident and Emergency departments, police stations or in another visible location in the community. The case studies below illustrate how this role would operate in practice.

Birmingham Acute Hospital Liaison Trust

This hospital trust provides a good example of enabling people with learning disabilities to access mainstream hospital care. The health facilitation project, provided by South Birmingham PCT, runs a team of two community nurses and three support workers provide support for patients and educate and advise staff. It was established to meet the concerns of local carers who felt that the local hospital poorly responded to people with learning disabilities. To date, anecdotal evidence suggests that it has been successful in allaying fears of going into hospital. (Glasby 2003)

Revolving Doors Agency Link Worker

This voluntary organisation provides an innovative approach to meeting the needs of ex-offenders, which illustrates how a service navigator would function. Link Workers were established in four London boroughs and in Buckinghamshire in 2000, with the aim of providing whole needs support to prevent offenders from going a continual journey through the revolving door to prison.

Concentrating on those who are typically hard to reach by services, the scheme targeted clients with mental health problems, drug dependency, homelessness and poor housing. They offered clients help with making benefit claims, access to health services, assistance with accommodation, as well as general advocacy and emotional support. In addition to providing a navigational role, Link Workers worked in teams and operated on the principle that there were no closed cases. Twenty four per cent of clients were deemed to experience 'improvement' in their life with the benefit of a Link Worker and none saw their situation get any worse. (Moran and O'Shea 2003, Revolving Doors Agency 2003)

Connected Care Centres: meeting complex needs

So far we have concentrated on universal reforms to improve service delivery, from changing the culture of health and social care to developing new professional roles. These are vital changes, but alone they are not enough to meet the complex needs of people who live in deprived communities. There is a need for a new way of delivering health and social care support in the context of the wider community. Our proposed model of Connected Care Centres will meet the needs of those who experience both breadth and depth of need and live in deprived communities. It should meet the needs of people who do not fulfil the specific criteria for any other service.

This new model of delivery enables policy makers to close the gap between health and social care solutions and social inclusion strategies. Connected Care Centres will be visible parts of the local community and their staff will be committed to assertive outreach work, in order to target those who are hardest to reach. Furthermore, people will be able to refer themselves to the service, rather than being dependent on other service providers to recommend them. The service will be designed and delivered for the local community by the local community. Connected Care Centres go hand-in-hand with a reformed commissioning process, which is vital to effective service design. Local commissioners will conduct a needs audit in order to assess the scale and the level of unmet need and work with service providers and users to determine the detailed structure of the local centre. The Connected Care Centres should draw up a local specification or care plan following the needs audit. The local care plan should be based on the needs and aspirations of local communities rather than what is currently available in terms of service provision. Commissioners will be responsible for monitoring the quality of the service and assessing whether it is successful in meeting the needs of the client group.

These Centres are based on a common approach for people with complex needs, rather than a fixed model and the exact specification of the Centre will vary according to the local needs audit. We have drawn on examples of existing good practice (some of which are cited here) to determine the common principles behind the new service model.

- Co-location of a variety of NHS, social care and voluntary professionals

- Common assessment procedure

- Established procedures for sharing information

- Shared training

- Single point of entry

- Round-the-clock support

- Managed transitions

- Continuing support

The Matrix, South Tyneside

The Matrix in South Tyneside provides an excellent example of how a complex needs service for young people operates in practice. Co-located under one roof is a network of key providers, including a drugs action team worker, an arrest referral worker, representatives from both health and housing authorities, a mental health nurse and a link to Connexions. There is a common assessment procedure and the team makes collective decisions about which worker is most appropriate to work with a particular client. Although setting up this one stop shop was not without challenges, group training and regular team meetings have helped staff at the Matrix to negotiate potential problems of different professional working practices (ippr interview).

Co-location

Co-located professionals would be the nucleus of a service to meet complex needs. Individual professionals would take lead responsibility for particular clients, but co-location would facilitate team strategies. The complex needs audit would determine more precisely which professional workers need to be part of the service. It is likely to include a range of NHS, social services and voluntary professionals. As the Matrix case study suggests, housing representatives and arrest referral workers are also likely candidates for a co-located centre. In order for co-location to be successful it should be underpinned by other strategies to meet whole needs, such as a common assessment procedure and established procedures for sharing information.

Common assessment procedure

Connected Care Centres will operate a common assessment procedure. This will evaluate the whole needs of the individual, irrespective of who will become their key worker. The procedure will assess health needs, social needs, as well as emotional needs. In practice, this means taking into account any past and current medical needs, current family situation, housing conditions, personal finance, employment, skills and plans for the future; it requires attention to people's interests, personality and cultural background. Common assessment will mean that people are not alienated by re-telling a difficult story many times over, or moved between different agencies for repeat assessments.

Established procedures for sharing information

Adult social care services would benefit from similar information, referral and tracking schemes that are currently being developed in Children's Services. (See Telford and Wrekin case studies below). Connected Care Centres need to work out their strategy for sharing information within the Centre, as well as making links with external agencies where possible. Although the issues of data protection and confidentiality remain important, they should not be used as a barrier to sharing information when this benefits the service outcome. The Turning Point North East Database system suggests how the balance between confidentiality and information sharing can be achieved.

Established procedures for sharing information should contribute to other desired outcomes. Better information sharing should also contribute to better understanding of whole needs across an area and ensure that information follows the person between services. Information and tracking systems can play a central role in promoting professional relationships between different partners, removing cultural barriers and providing a mechanism for monitoring and evaluating interventions. It would also support a common assessment procedure, by avoiding repeat assessment and referral.

Telford and Wrekin's AWARE IRT system

This is an Information, Referral and Tracking (IRT) System designed to safeguard children at risk, so they are not lost to the authorities. Highlighted in Every Child Matters, AWARE rests on clear protocols for sharing information. The system was developed through a range of locally based protocols to ensure that information is used confidentially and appropriately. Similar IRT systems are due to be introduced nationwide from September 2004 for Children's Trusts. (www.telford.gov.uk)

Turning Point North East Database system
The North East Database is an extranet system that covers five areas: Newcastle, Gateshead, South Tyneside, North Tyneside and Sunderland. With the aim of ensuring that information follows the individual, the database is an information sharing system between different statutory and voluntary agencies. Partners include commissioners, Drug Action Teams, the police, probation services, health and social services. The system records the numbers of people seen via arrest referral, numbers of people referred into treatment and numbers in treatment. It is accessed by all partners and linked to national targets and has been judged to contribute to improved professional relations. In order to ensure the rights of the service user, consent of individual is sought from the outset and protection of the identity of the individual is assured.

Training

Professionals working in Connected Care Centres need to have joint training across health, social care, housing and employment issues. However, this does not mean that frontline workers have to strive towards the impossible goal of becoming experts on all aspects of health and social care as well as housing and employment services. Co-location would encourage a sharing of expertise and would help to develop multi-agency working. Ultimately, having the right range of skills, as well as the willingness to explore creative solutions, is more important than limitless knowledge. As one service manager commented: 'You need to be a jack of all trades. It's about having the knowledge and equipment to deal with a range of problems' (Edwards 2003).

Professionals working in Connected Care Centres need to possess 'joining skills', namely the ability to work effectively in a problem solving partnership with users. Firstly, this requires empathy and the flexibility to respond to the user's own motivation. Secondly, workers would require 'intervention skills', such as the ability to reframe a problem as it is commonly perceived, as well as a level of creative thinking (Smale 2000). Thirdly, professionals working with people with complex needs would need the skills to respond to people who are vulnerable, may lack confidence or have challenging behaviour.

Single point of entry

Connected Care Centres provide a single point of entry into a targeted intervention and access to wider support network offered by mainstream services. Discussions with stakeholders expressed some concern that a 'complex needs service' could exclude people from mainstream services. In fact, Connected Care Centres should operate as a mechanism for better linking people into mainstream services, by enabling people to access mainstream housing and employment services.

Southwark Intensive Parenting Project, Southwark & Maudsley NHS Trust

Predating Sure Start, this is a parenting advice service offered by the mental health services trust. Local health visitors and school nurses visit families to offer a package of treatment in relation to their particular needs. They help parents who have children with challenging behaviour, when the parent themselves may have a mental health problems, or drug or alcohol problems.

In accordance with this multi-disciplinary approach the services accepts referrals from CAMHS and the Community Drug Action Project. (Day 2002)

Round-the-clock support

Connected Care Centres will offer direct access so that people can refer themselves to the service without necessarily being referred from another agency. Round-the-clock support is crucial so people get help in a crisis and to ensure they get the support they need quickly. However 24-hour services also fulfil a more general emotional support for people with complex needs in relation to accommodation, employment, training, education, personal finance and health matters. ippr's research highlighted a lack of out-of-hours support.

> Detox is good but when you come out, the aftercare is the main thing that's lacking...like after 6pm at night there's nothing, that's when you've got to deal with it. I remember being relieved after 11pm because I knew the off-licences were shut and there was nowhere I could buy a drink (Edwards 2003).

Managed transitions

Connected Care Centres fall into an aged-based approach for services, but need to attend to service boundaries, both at the upper and lower age range. Connected Care Centres should incorporate bridge building services to accommodate the needs of people at transition points, and should form part of a 'whole life network' of social care support.

Continual support

There would be no closed cases in Connected Care Centres. The Centre would offer clients support at any time in their lives, whether the individual was seeking help preventing relapse, coping in a new job or experiencing difficulties or in any other scenario. By virtue of working in the community and maintaining high visibility, Connected Care professionals would be more approachable if further interventions were needed.

We recommend that the Government invests in and pilots Connected Care Centres in some of the country's most deprived neighbourhoods.

11. Conclusion: a strategy for reform

Key recommendations

As we have suggested there is no single solution to meeting complex needs. It requires a multi-faceted strategy with participation from government, commissioners, local providers and service users. The key elements of a strategy for transforming social care services are:

- A recognition of whole needs – physical, social and emotional – should be at the centre of social care objectives and services;

- A statutory duty should be placed on the NHS and local authorities to collect data and monitor multiple service use;

- The commissioning process must be strengthened by a clearer definition of roles and better training to ensure a more strategic approach is taken;

- A level playing field should be created between different sectors, including longer-term and standard contracts for the voluntary sector;

- All professionals who interact with people with complex needs should be trained to recognise and relate effectively with people with complex needs;

- A new professional role of 'service navigator' should be explored to help provide case management, advocacy and support;

- An understanding that purposeful cultural change is more important than further structural reform;

- Connected Care Centres should be piloted in deprived neighbourhoods.

The need to act

Failure to meet complex needs carries a significant human cost and this alone suggests a new approach to service delivery is needed. Meeting complex needs promises health and social care services that are more effective services as well as more efficient services. Our strategy for reform will help extend the public service reform agenda to those who are hardest to reach and deliver social inclusion for those who are hardest to help. Yet, ultimately meeting complex needs is not a minority issue, as it should help transform social care services for everyone.

Bibliography

Adams R (2002) *Social Policy for Social Work* Palgrave

Allen D (2002) 'Tackling the Complex Needs of Asylum Seekers' *Primary Care 4*

Arblaster L *et al* (1998) *Achieving the Impossible – Interagency collaboration to aid the housing, health and social care needs of people able to live in or housing* Joseph Rowntree Foundation/Policy Press

Audit Commission (2002) *Changing Habits – The commissioning and management of community drug treatment services for adults* Audit Commission, London.

Bamford T (2001) *Commissioning and Purchasing* Routledge

Billis D and Glennerster H (1998) 'Human Services and the Voluntary Sector: Towards a theory of comparative advantage' *Journal of Social Policy 27*

Brett W and Schofield J (2002) 'Integrated Care Pathways for Patients with Complex Needs' *Nursing Standard 16*

Boyd D (1999) 'Multiple Needs and Multiple Gaps' *Addiction Today 10*

Boyle K and Jenkins C (2003) *Housing for Londoners with Mental Health needs – A review of recent developments* The Kings Fund

Bubb S (2003) *Replacing the State? The case for third sector delivery* Association of Chief Executives of the Voluntary Sector

Cameron M *et al* (2003) *Community Renewal and Mental Health – Strengthening the links* The Kings Fund/National Institute for Mental Health in England

Commission for Health Improvement (2003) *What CHI has Found in Mental Health Trusts* London

Commission on Public Private Partnerships (2001) *Building Better Partnerships* ippr

Compass Partnership (2002) *Mental Health Services in the Voluntary Sector* Mental Health Providers Network.

Corry D and Stoker G (2002) *New Localism: Refashioning the centre-local relationship* New Local Government Network 2002

Cotterill L and Barr W (2000) *Targeting in Mental Health Services – A multi-disciplinary challenge* Ashgate Publishing

Davies J and Morgan H (2003) 'Meeting Mental Health Needs – Count us in!' *Learning Disability Practice 6*

Day C (2002) 'Children and Young People with Complex Needs' *Community Practitioner 75*

Dean H (2002) *A Different Deal? Welfare to work for people with multiple problems and needs*

Department for Education and Skills (2003) *Every Child Matters* The Stationery Office

Department of Health (2003) *The NHS Contractors' Companion* Available at www.doh.gov.uk/commissioning

Department of Health (2002) *Mental health – dual diagnosis good practice guide* The Stationery Office

Department of Health (2001a) *Delivering the NHS Plan* The Stationery Office

Department of Health (2001b) *Valuing People: A new strategy for learning disability in the 21st century* The Stationery Office

Department of Health (2001c) *National Service Framework for Older People – Executive Summary* The Stationery Office

Department of Health (2000a) *The NHS Plan: a plan for investment, a plan for reform* The Stationery Office

Department of Health (2000b) *Vulnerable Young People and Drugs – Opportunities to tackle inequalities* The Stationery Office

Department of Health (1999a) *Effective Care Coordination in Mental Health Services: Modernizing the CPA – policy booklet* The Stationery Office

Department of Health (1999b) *National Service Framework for Mental Health* The Stationery Office

Department of Health (1998a) *Modernising Social Services* The Stationery Office

Department of Health (1998b) *Modernising Mental Health Services* The Stationery Office

Dunn S (1999) *Creating Accepting Communities: Report of the MIND Inquiry into Social Exclusion and Mental Health* MIND

Edwards L (2003) *What do service users think? – A qualitative research study* MS www.ippr.org.uk

Edwards L and Hatch B (2003) *Passing Time – A report about young people and communities* ippr

Fletcher P (2000) *Social Inclusion for Vulnerable People – Linking regeneration and community care* PFA/Housing Corporation/ Nuffield Institute for Health

Gilbert P (2003) *The Value of Everything – Social work and its importance in the field of mental health* Russell House Publications.

Glasby A (2003) 'Access all Areas' *Learning Disability Practice 6*

Glasby J and Peck E (2003) *Care Trusts: Partnership working in action* Routledge

Glendinning *et al* (2000) 'New Kinds of Care, New Kinds of Relationships: How purchasing services affects relationships in giving and receiving personal assistance' *Health & Social Care in the Community 7*

Glendinning, Powell and Rummery (2002) *National Evaluation of Freedoms & Flexibilities*

Goodinge S (2000) *A Jigsaw of Services* Inspection of Services to Support Adults in their Parenting Role, Department of Health and Social Services Inspectorate

Griffiths S (2000) *Supporting People All the Way – An overview of the supporting people programme* Joseph Rowntree Foundation

Greatly A and Ford R (2002) *Out of the Maze – Reaching and supporting Londoners with severe mental health problems* Kings Fund/The Sainsbury Centre for Mental Health.

Greig R and Poxton R (2001) 'Nice Process – But did Joint Commissioning Change Anyone's Life' *Managing Community Care 2001; 9*

Jenkins G (1999) 'Coping with Complex Needs: Managing Competing Demands' *Housing, Care and Community Support 2*

Jordan B and Jordan C (2001) *Social Work and the Third Way – Tough love as social policy* Sage

Harker L (2003) *Dimensions of Poverty and Social Exclusion – Persistence of childhood poverty* MS

Hayes G (2003) *Getting it Right for Young People – a vision for young people's social care* Turning Point

Henwood M (2001) *Future Imperfect? Report of the Kings Fund Care & Support Inquiry* The Kings Fund

Heyman P, Swain J and Gillmann M (2004) 'Organisational simplification and secondary complexity in health services for adults with learning disabilities' *Social Science and Medicine 58*

Hill M (ed) *Local Authority Social Services* Oxford (2000)

Home Office (2002) *Updated Drugs Strategy* The Stationery Office

Homeless Link (2003) *Briefing Bridge the Gap – Multiple needs campaign* Available at www.homeless.org.uk

Homeless Link (2003a) *Older Homeless People with Multiple Needs* Available at www.homeless.org.uk

Homeless Link (2003b) *Briefing on Personality Crisis* Available at www.homeless.org.uk

Homeless Link (2003c) *Submission to the Mental Health Committee on NHS Mental Health Services* www.homeless.org.uk

Howard League for Penal Reform (2003) *Busy Doing Nothing: The Experience of 18-20 year old men on remand* Available at www.howardleague.org/publications

Hudson B (2000) *The Changing Role of Social Care*

Keene J (2001) *Clients with Complex Needs* Blackwell Science

Kendall L and Harker L (2002) (eds) *From Welfare to Wellbeing – The future of Social Care* IPPR

Kendall L and Lissauer R (2003) *The Future Healthcare Worker* IPPR

Klee H, McLean and Yarkovsky C (2002) *Employing Drug Users: Individual and systematic barriers to rehabilitation* Joseph Rowntree Foundation

Knapp M *et al* (1999) 'Private, Voluntary or Public? Comparative cost effectiveness in community mental health care' *Policy and Politics 27*

Lakey J, Barnes M and Parry J (2001) *Getting a Chance: Employment support for young people with multiple disadvantages* Joseph Rowntree Foundation

Lester H (2003) *Cases for Change: An overview of the evidence which is driving the agenda for change* National Institute for Mental Health in England

Light D and Cohen A (2003) *Commissioning Mental Health Services* The Sainsbury Centre for Mental Health

Lindsey M (2000) 'Services for People with Learning Disability and Mental Health Problems' *Mental Health Review 5*

Local Government Association, Association of Directors of Social Services (2002) *All Our Tomorrows – Inverting the triangle of care* LGA/ADSS

Maclean Steel K and Palmer C (2000) *Improving the care of people in substance misuse services* Royal College of Psychiatrists

McCall M and Cockersall P (2003) *Mental Health and Social Exclusion Consultation* St Mungos

McCall M and Cockersall P (2002) *Trigger Points to Homelessness: Effective preventative action* St Mungos

McGregor *et al* (2003) *Developing People – Regenerating place: achieving greater integration for Local Area Based Regeneration* Joseph Rowntree Foundation

Moran L and O'Shea N (2000) *Mental Health, Multiple Needs and the Police – Findings from the Revolving Doors link agency scheme*

Morris J (1999) *Hurtling into a void – transition to adulthood for young disabled people 'with complex health and support needs'* Joseph Rowntree Foundation

Morris J (2000) *'That Kind of Life?' Social exclusion and young disabled people with high levels of support needs* Scope

National Institute for Mental Health in England (2003) *The Role of Values in Mental Health* NIMHE

Parry Jones B (2001) 'Needs-Led Assessment: the Challenges and the Reality' *Health and Social Care in the Community 9*

Perkins R, Repper J (1998) *Dilemmas in Community Mental Health Practice: Choice or control* Abingdon

Peterson T (1998) 'Is Dual Diagnosis a useful term?' *Nursing Times 94*

Piachaud/Sutherland (2002) *Changing Poverty Post-1997* Centre for Analysis of Social Exclusion (CASE)

Policy Studies Institute (1989) *Seebohm Twenty Years On: Three stages in the Development of Personal Social Services*

Poxton R (1999) *Partnerships in Primary and Social Care – Integrating services for vulnerable people* The Kings Fund

Robbins B (2000) 'Labels and Service Delivery for People with Learning Disability' *The Mental Health Review 5*

Peck E and Leat D (2003) *A Voluntary Finance Initiative: Benefits and proposals* Health Services Management Centre, MS

Peck E *et al* (2003) *Developing New Forms of Capital Finance for Voluntary Organisations* Health Services Management Centre, MS.

Peck E *et al* (2001) 'The Meanings of "Culture" in Health and Social Care: A Case Study of the Combined Trust in Somerset' *Journal of Interprofessional Care 15*

Rassool G (2002) *Dual diagnosis – Substance Misuse and Psychiatric Disorders* Blackwell Science

Reed Z (1994) *Health and Social Care: What future for joint planning?* Camden Social Services Department

Revolving Doors Agency (2003a) *Snakes and Ladders: Findings from the Revolving Doors Agency Link Worker Scheme* RDA

Revolving Doors Agency (2003b) *Where do they go? Mental Health, Housing and Leaving Prison* RDA, The Kings Fund

Royal College of Psychiatrists (1997) *A Manifesto for Mental Health: Rebuilding mental health services for the 21st century*

Sainsbury Centre for Mental Health (2002) *Breaking the Circles of Fear – A review of the relationship between mental health services and African and Caribbean communities*

Sainsbury Centre for Mental Health (2001) *Setting the Standard – The new agenda for Primary Care Organisations commissioning mental health services*

Sainsbury Centre for Mental Health (2000) *Taking your Partners – Using opportunities for inter agency partnership in mental health*

Sainsbury Centre for Mental Health (1998) *Keys to Engagement – Review of care for people with severe mental illness who are hard to engage with services*

Salvage (2002) *Rethinking Professionalism- the first step for patient focused care* MS Available at www.ippr.org.uk

Save the Children (2003) *Britain's Poorest Children*

Seebohm F (1968) Report of the committee on local authority and allied personal social services HMSO

Simons K and Russell O *A Summary of Findings from 'Crossing the Line' – a Research Project on the Interface between Mental Health and Learning Disability Services*

Smale G, Tusan G and Stratham D (2002) *Social Work and Social Problems*

Shelter (2004) *The Act in Action: An assessment of homelessness reviews and strategies*

Social Exclusion Unit (2003) *Briefing Paper on Mental Health and Social Exclusion* The Stationery Office

Social Exclusion Unit (2002) *Reducing Reoffending by Ex-Offenders-Summary Version* The Stationery Office

Social Exclusion Unit (2001) *A New Commitment to Neighbourhood Renewal – National Strategy Action Plan* The Stationery Office

Social Exclusion Unit (1998) *Bring Britain Together: A National Strategy for Neighbourhood Renewal* The Stationery Office

Social Services Inspectorate (2003) *Modern Social Services: A commitment to the future* The 12th Annual Report of the Chief Inspector of Social Services 2002/2003, The Stationery Office

Stanley K and Regan S (2003) *The Missing Million – Supporting disabled people into work* ippr

St Mungos (2003) *Mental Health and Social Exclusion Consultation* MS

Tanti V and Blackman G (2001) 'A Partnership Scheme for People with Complex Needs' *Nursing Times 97*

Timmins N (2001) *The Five Giants – A biography of the welfare state* Harper Collins

Turning Point (2003) *Briefing Paper on a Standard Form of Contract* MS

Virgo N *et al* (2001) 'The prevalence and characteristics of co-occuring serious mental illness and substance abuse or dependence in the patients of adult mental health and addictions services in East Dorset' *Journal of Mental Health 10*

Watkins T *et al* (2001) *Dual Diagnosis – An Integrated Approach to treatment* Sage

Wanless D (2002) *Securing Our Future Health – Taking a long term view* HM Treasury, The Stationery Office

Weaver T and Ritter D (1999) *Report of a Study into the Prevalence and Management of Clients with Mental Illness and Substance Misuse Co-Morbidity in the London Borough of Hammersmith and Fulham* Imperial College

Weston J (2002) *Choosing, Getting and Keeping a Job: A study of supported employment for people with complex needs* Scottish Human Services Trust

Whitehouse K (1999) 'Rethinking Service Relationships; Partners or protagonists' *Housing, Care and Community Support 2*

Appendix 1: ippr qualitative research with service users

In Autumn 2003, ippr conducted qualitative research with service users who were in touch with Turning Point services. Specifically, the research explored the 'journey' that service users go through in order to access the services they need, service user accounts of what works and what doesn't work and relationships with service providers. Service managers were also involved in these conversations. Six different services were visited together and the discussions included informal group meetings and more intensive individual interviews.

Project	Details	Research
The Mill	6-bedded residential unit in Leyland, Lancashire which houses young people who are homeless or at risk of homelessness. It offers 24-hour support on site.	Discussion group with 3 young residents, informal conversations with staff and interview with service manager
The Crossing	Community Drug and Alcohol service for the London Borough of Barnet. Offers a range of services including one-to-one, key working, drop-ins and group-work.	2 interviews with service users, each lasting around an hour and a half. Interview with service manager.
ACAPS	Works with 10-25 year olds in Lambeth, Southwark and Lewisham. Services include counselling, drug education, community outreach and health training. Every member of staff is a qualified substance misuse worker.	1 interview with a service user and lengthy interview with service manager and worker.
Focus Point	Day centre and outreach team working with people with learning disabilities in Salisbury. Creates individual care packages for its service users, many of whom are seen to be 'challenging'.	Short discussions with 3 service users, interview with service manager and observation work and informal discussion with other members of staff.
Gwydir and Huntingdon Project	Provides a community service based on an assertive outreach model for up to 60 people across South and West Cambridgeshire. Whilst, primarily a mental health service, service users experience a wide range of needs including drug and alcohol use, self-harm and eating disorders.	Interviews with 5 service users, most were conducted in their own home. Informal discussion with service manager.
Birmingham Drugline	Birmingham Drugline works with people who are misusing drugs. Staff work with anyone affected by substance misuse, along with family, friends, and carers of users.	Interviews with 7 service users, lasting between 20 minutes and an hour and a half.